Childless by Choice:

A Feminist Anthology

edited by

Irene Reti

Printed in the United States of America by McNaughton and Gunn. ISBN: 0-939821-03-6.

"Choosing Childlessness" by Randi Locke first appeared in *The Reporter*, the magazine of Women's American ORT. "On Not Having Children" by Michele Patenaude was originally published in December of 1987 in *Vermont Woman*, a now-defunct monthly women's newspaper. "Artemis" by Eloise Klein Healy was first published in 1991 in *Artemis in Echo Park* by Firebrand Books, Ithaca, New York and is reprinted with permission of the author and publisher. "Motherhood: Reclaiming the Demon Texts" first appeared in *Ms.* Magazine, May/June 1991. "Childlessness" by Joyce Goldenstern will appear in *Sojourner*, October 1992.

Acknowledgements

I would like to dedicate this book to my mother, Ingrid Reti, who did not have the same choices I have, who has been my feminist inspiration since my teenage years, and who has always supported my choice not to have children.

Special thanks also to Julia Chapin, copyeditor and proofreader extraordinaire.

Contents

Introduction

Childless. Child-free. Nullipara. Not-Mothers. Even language fails us, we women who have chosen not to have children. We live in the negative, in the absence, always on the defensive.

I write these words as the Supreme Court of the United States is poised to overturn Roe vs. Wade, to decide the future of women's reproductive rights. The right to choose not to have children at all is an integral part of women's reproductive freedom, and should be a fundamental part of a feminist agenda. Yet, as Ann Snitow writes here in her article "Motherhood: Reclaiming the Demon Texts," "It's been some time since feminists demanding abortion have put front and center the idea that one good use to which one might put this right is to choose not to have kids at all. Chastised in the Reagan years, pro-choice strategists understandably have emphasized the right to wait, to space one's children, to have each child wanted. They feared invoking any image that could be read as withdrawal from the role of nurturer."

Feminism has betrayed childless women. "A maternal revivalism has occurred over the past two decades within feminism as well as in the dominant culture," writes Carolyn Morell. This romanticization of motherhood also extends to the lesbian community, and many lesbians included in this book write about the pressure they feel to participate in "the lesbian baby boom."

This book is feminist in intent and content. It seeks to put the choice not to have children in the context of women's reproductive freedom. The writing here is by women of diverse backgrounds and ages—working class and middle class; Jewish, Chicana, Euro-American, African American, Native American; lesbian and heterosexual; rural and urban.

The choice not to mother is a complex. This book reflects that complexity and refuses to smooth over the ambivalence and sadness that childless women may feel. In Lesléa Newman's story "Of Balloons and Bubbles," a woman who has taken her friend's little girl out for an afternoon at a pumpkin festival says, "I stroke her back and she sighs contentedly, clinging to me as my heart turns over, heavy with the dearness of her and the weight of my choice." Alison Solomon's poem "An Empty Womb" describes her long struggle to accept her infertility and remain childless, rather than pursue other options for becoming a mother. "I have never seen a poem/suggesting/that periods are a state of mind./That even an empty womb/is beautiful."

Ethnicity adds another dimension to the difficult decision about whether to have children. In Terri de la Peña's story "Nullipara, 44," the main character tells another Chicana that she doesn't want to have children. "The Latina stares as if I have uttered a blasphemy. And, coming from the same Catholic-steeped culture she undoubtedly was raised in, I suppose I have." "The imperative to 'go forth and multiply' was inherent in my Jewish upbringing," writes Randi Locke. "It's awfully hard to meet another Indian," writes mixed-blood Cahuilla Valerie Chase. "And I don't see the point in putting a non-Indian in the world."

For many women the choice not to have children is integrally connected with artistic expression. We do not have illusions about the challenge of continuing to lead a creative life while raising babies. "I have made choices [my mother] finds incomprehensible. I call myself Chicana, lesbian, feminist, writer," writes Terri de la Peña. "At forty-four, she had her fifth child; I have just finished my first novel." Valerie Chase, classical violinist and violist writes, "I thought, oh my God, I can't even think of having a child because for the first time in my life I was really making a lot of musical progress." "What would have to be true before you would be ready to have a baby?" asks Elissa Raffa. "I would have to be willing to spend one third of my income on daycare. I would have to be willing to raise a son. I would have to be willing to put my writing, political activism, and other commitments on hold for a few years. I would lose the freedom to say yes to anything that comes my way."

To be childless is to be accused of being self-centered, selfish. In the truest sense of the word the women in this book *are* self-ish. "There is nothing new or unusual about this/her mother or grandmother must have done it also/I, wide-eyed observer, took note, and vowed/when I was grown, to pour/but one glass only, and that my own." (Stephanie Harris) Yet, the women in this book have a passionate desire to contribute to the world. "I will overpopulate the world/with chiming consonants,/leave images red and wailing/on the doorsteps of the unsuspecting,/breed metaphors that fill the night/with flesh of chutzpah/and bone of hope." (Paula Amann)

Perhaps childless women are some of the women who might have made the best mothers, for many of us are fully cognizant of what a responsibility motherhood is. Eloise Klein Healy writes "The first thing a child should see/is the pink sunrise of a nipple, not the green wind/of a branch whipping in passing."

The final reason many women cite for not having children is ecological. In "Saving the Earth One Less Baby at a Time" Michele Patenaude writes, "You can compost, recycle, carpool and put bricks

2

in your toilet tank until the cows come home, and it won't compare to the environmental benefits of bringing one less child into the world." Patenaude emphasizes that it is the children, the people of the industrialized world who are consuming the majority of the resources of the planet, and thus avoids the racist pitfall of blaming third world women for the world's ecological degradation.

The purpose of this book is not to devalue women who have children. Both childless women and women who mother are oppressed. But much has been written about the difficulties of mothering under patriarchy. This collection seeks to illuminate the lives of those of us who do not mother. As Janet Aalfs puts it in her poem "what's been done,"

what's been done
by my mother
and hers before
is why I'm here
but the ones that didn't

who are they

This is who we are—proud, complex, creative, dignified and diverse women. I hope this book is useful in helping any woman choose whether or not to have children, no matter what she ultimately decides to do with her life. For those of us who have chosen not to mother, I hope this anthology takes us off the defensive and affirms our brave, independent, and fertile lives.

—Irene Reti, July 2, 1992

Janet E. Aalfs

what's been done

what's been done
by my mother
and hers before
is why I'm here
but the ones that didn't

who are they

every day the gasp
of legs open
to shining naked
heads their crested
entries into light

their shrieks

of done it again
like a sock turned
newside out
time and time until
at me the hand stops

whose child will I wear

but my own
self laughing into the mirror
of my own self laughing
into the mirror of
my own self

Ann Snitow

Motherhood—Reclaiming the Demon Texts

At 47, I have no children, a fact that has gradually changed its social meaning as I, and the feminist movement, grow older together. Recently, I began to wonder whether feminism is trying to resist the flood of pronatalism in which I now live—or does it sometimes add to it? It seemed time for a bout of reading—a wide, eclectic sampling of what modern U.S. feminism has had to say about motherhood.

If I hoped to find a strong and clear critique of the prescription that all women must mother, what I found instead was a growing crisis of authority: who is allowed to criticize pronatalism or to question the desire for children? The mothers feel it disingenuous to take on this task; they have their children after all. And the childless are easily made to feel their critique is a species of sour grapes. Does the lesbian community speak up with unembarrassed enthusiasm for the child-free life? Not now. Far more typical at the moment is the recent book *Politics of the Heart: A Lesbian Parenting Anthology*. Not even the mothers who had children against their will are in a position to complain; they fear it will hurt the children to know they were unwanted.

My reading showed that feminism set out to break these narrative taboos—those surrounding the mothers and the nonmothers—but for a variety of reasons we were better able to attend to mothers' voices than we were able to imagine a full life without motherhood. To see how this asymmetry emerged, I've begun to construct a time line of feminism on motherhood. Though the record is complex, I see three distinct periods along the time line. First, 1963 (Friedan, of course) to about 1974—the period of what I call the "demon texts," for which we have been apologizing ever since. Second, 1975-1979, the period in which feminism tries to take on the issue of motherhood, to criticize the institution, explore the actual experience, theorize the social and psychological implications. By 1979, in a massive shift in the politics of the whole country, some feminist work shifts, too, from discussing motherhood to discussing families. The feminist hope of breaking the iron bond between mother and child seems gone, except in rhetorical flourishes, perhaps gone for good in this wave.

I'm going to try—briefly—to substantiate this periodization, but first a reminder: the particular piece of feminist intellectual history I'm exploring here follows quite closely the trajectory of the baby boom generation, what demographers call the mouse in the python, a large bulge traveling down the decades. The culture this group

5

creates, including the culture of feminism, shapes the era I'm describing here. For the young, the next bit of the line remains a mystery. Current debates about the real meaning of black teenage pregnancy and the low rate of marriage and fertility among college students give hints of how women may now be experimenting with the placement of children in their life cycles. It's a cheerful thought that many of you will have experiences and ideas about what motherhood means that don't correspond to this outline.

Period I, 1963 to About 1974

1963 is the year of *The Feminine Mystique*. The inadequacies of that book are well known. Many have criticized Friedan's classism, racism, homophobia, her false universals. But Friedan herself has ignored all this and criticized *The Feminine Mystique* herself on different grounds altogether. In *The Second Stage* (1981), Friedan blames her earlier book for being antifamily, for trying to pry women away from children, and for overemphasizing women as autonomous individuals. In fact, *The Feminine Mystique* is rather mild on these points. But it is the first of my "demon texts," by which I mean books demonized, apologized for, endlessly quoted out of context, to prove that the feminism of the early seventies was, in Friedan's words of recantation, "strangely blind."

The most famous demon text is Shulamith Firestone's *The Dialectic of Sex: The Case for Feminist Revolution* (1970). This book is usually the starting point for discussions of how feminism has been "strangely blind" about motherhood. Certainly there are few of its sentences that Firestone would leave unmodified if she were writing with the same intent today. Her undertheorized enthusiasm for cybernetics, her self-hating disgust at the pregnant body ("Pregnancy is barbaric"), her picture of the female body as a prison from which a benign, nonpatriarchal science might release us have all dated. Finally, though, it's her tone we can't identify with, the atmosphere of freewheeling, shameless speculation. *The Dialectic of Sex* is an example of utopian writing, and part of the demonizing of this text arises out of a misreading of genre. Everyone colludes in calling it a mother-hating book. Search the pages. You won't find the evidence. Firestone's work is reactive and rhetorical. The point is always "smash patriarchy," not mothers.

Of course there are real demon texts inside feminism, callow works like a few of the essays in the collection *Pronatalism: The Myth of Mom and Apple Pie* (1974), which reject childbearing in favor of having unsoiled white rugs and the extra cash to buy them. But such moments are rare. In my search for early feminist mother-hating what I found was—mostly—an absence. In the major anthologies like *Sisterhood is Powerful, Women in Sexist Society*, and *Liberation Now!* there are hardly any articles on any aspect of mothering. Nothing strange, really, about this. The mouse had only just started down the python; most of the writers were young.

The *Our Bodies/Ourselves* that was a newsprint booklet in 1971 reflects a time when feminism had established a harsh self-questioning about motherhood. Under "Pregnancy," one finds such things as: "We, as women, grow up in a society that subtly leads us to believe that we will find our ultimate fulfillment by living out our reproductive function . . ." But soon, very soon, this preemptory and radical questioning was misread as an attack on housewives. This has been as effective an instance of divide and conquer as I know. By the late seventies, both the mothers and the nonmothers were on the defensive. What a triumph of backlash.

Period II, 1975-1979

With the glossy *Ourselves and Our Children* of 1978, we find ourselves in a different feminist world. The book acknowledges that "until quite recently" having a baby wasn't really considered a decision, but then goes on to assume that now all that has changed, ending with this gee-whiz sentence: "Now almost 5 percent of the population has declared its intentions to remain child-free." This is a liberal text, celebrating variety without much concern for uneven consequences. Both people who have decided to have children and people who have decided against are quoted at some length, but the structural result is an aimless pluralism, a series of lifestyle questions, no politics.

But if I'm using the word liberal pejoratively, this, my second period, is also liberal in the best sense of the word: a time of freer speech, wider inquiry, a refusal of orthodoxy, an embrace of the practical reality. In these years, the feminist work of exploring motherhood took off: 1976 alone saw the publication of Adrienne Rich's *Of Woman Born*, Dorothy Dinnerstein's *The Mermaid and the Minotaur*, Jane Lazarre's *The Mother Knot*, and Linda Gordon's *Women's Body, Women's Right*. Also in that year French feminism began to be a power in feminist academic thinking in the United States. *Signs* published Hélène Cixous' "The Laugh of the Medusa," which included these immediately controversial words: "There is always within [woman] at least a little of that good mother's milk. She writes in white ink." Mysteries and provocations—which introduced a flood!

7

1978: Nancy Chodorow's *The Reproduction of Mothering* and Michele Wallace's *Black Macho and the Myth of the Superwoman*. These books were events. The intellectual work of feminism has its renaissance in these years.

In her introduction to a brilliant special issue of *Feminist Studies* on motherhood in 1978, Rachel Blau DuPlessis honored what Adrienne Rich was trying to do in *Of Woman Born*—to pry mothering away from the patriarchal institution, motherhood. But then, DuPlessis went on to worry that Rich might be overreacting, over-privileging the body. "If, by the process of touching physicality," DuPlessis wrote, "Rich wants to find that essence beyond conflict, the place where all women necessarily meet, the essence of a woman, pure blood, I cannot follow there." Discussions like these inaugurate our continuing debates about essentialism, the body, and social construction.

DuPlessis asks the larger political question that nags throughout the period: Which construction of motherhood is productive for feminist work? If we take Dinnerstein at her word, we're trying to get men to be mothers. If we follow Rich, our energies move toward building a female culture capable of the support not only of women but also of their children. Feminist theory is still far from sorting out the implications for activism.

It's important to add, though, that right in the middle of this period, in 1977, the first Hyde Amendment was passed; we lost Medicaid abortion. Abortion—the primal scene of this wave—won to our amazement in 1973, was only affordable for all classes for four years before this right began slipping away.

Period III

My second period ends—and my third begins—with the brilliant threshold article by Sara Ruddick in 1980, "Maternal Thinking." Ruddick took seriously the question of what women actually do when they mother. She developed a rich description of what she called "maternal practice" and "maternal thinking," and her much reprinted article has been read, misread, appropriated into a variety of arguments. Is motherhood really a separable practice? Are its special features capable of translation into women's public power? Does motherhood also have the universality Ruddick's work implies? Does the different voices argument (also developed by Carol Gilligan in 1981) lead to a vigorous feminist politics?

Ruddick provides one of the best descriptions feminism has of why women are so deeply committed to the mothering experience, even under very oppressive conditions. Her work is a song to motherhood—multiphonic, without sugar—but still a song. "Maternal Thinking" is the fullest response since Adrienne Rich to the call to end my first taboo, the taboo on speaking the life of the mother. It leaves my other taboo, the viability of the choice not to mother, untouched, but this might well have seemed benign neglect in any other year but 1980. It was not part of Ruddick's intention to publish her work in the same year Reagan was elected, yet the meeting of the twain is, I think, part of this small history of feminism on motherhood.

Ruddick argues—with much reason—that hers is an anti-Reagan text: it includes men as mothers; it includes lesbians as mothers; it demands public support for women's work. But it is extremely difficult to do an end run around Reaganism by a mere proliferation of family forms. The left tried it; feminism tried it; everyone failed. (I'm thinking of Michael Lerner's Friends of Families organizing. I'm thinking of NOW's 1979 Assembly on the Future of the Family. I'm thinking of Betty Friedan in *The Second Stage.)* Women, not families, continue to do almost all domestic work.

My time line for the eighties is a record of frustration, re-trenchment, defeat, and sorrow. Out of the Baby M case in 1986-87 comes Phyllis Chesler's *Sacred Bond,* the very title unthinkable a decade earlier. Certainly things weren't going our way, and the stud-ies to prove it poured out. We get Chesler on the injustice of child cus-tody laws and Lenore Weitzman's frightening figures about what happens to women after no-fault divorce.

1986: my peak year for backlash, at least partially internalized by feminism, gives us Sue Miller's novel *The Good Mother* and Sylvia Ann Hewlett's *A Lesser Life.* In this particularly mean season, in which mothers do everything without social supports, Hewlett wants protection. Once a self-defined feminist, she sees nothing but liberal blarney in legal equality models. Hewlett blames feminism for not making demands on the state. Of course we did make them. One might argue that Hewlett's assumption that women will inevitably do most of the child-rearing is broadly shared by the men in power, too, and that this attitude itself is one reason it is hard to coerce the state to do the work.

There are exceptions to backlash thinking on the eighties time line—Rosalind Petchesky in her 1984 book on abortion for one—though several turned out to be books and articles published else-where. (I find my line doesn't work for other countries.) And however raggedly, women are already living out basically new story lines, making piecemeal changes. But on the political front, it's been some time since feminists demanding abortion have put front and center the idea that one good use to which one might put this right is to choose not to have kids at all. Chastised in the Reagan years, pro-choice strategists understandably have emphasized the right to wait, to space one's children, to have each child wanted. They feared invoking any image that could be read as a female withdrawal from the role of nurturer. We are—in this period of reaction—elaborating, extending, reinstitutionalizing motherhood for ourselves. Never has the baby been so delicious. A feminist theorist tells me she is more proud of her new baby than of all her books.

I don't mean to criticize these deep sentiments but to situate them. In 1970, feminist mothers, like all mothers, were briefly on the defensive, and ecstatic descriptions of mothering were themselves taboo. But now, since 1980, we have apologized again and again for ever having uttered a callow, classist, immature, or narcissistic word against mothering. Instead, we have praised the heroism of women raising children alone, or poor, usually both. We have embraced nurturance, sometimes wishing that men would share this ethic without much hoping they will, and we have soldiered on, caring for the kids (more first children were born in 1988 than in any year on record) and continuing to do 82 percent of the housework. Complaints now have a way of sounding monstrous, even to our own ears.

In backlash times like these it's easy for feminism's opponents to insist that anger at oppression is really anger at children or at mothers. The New Right has been brilliant at encouraging this slippage. Guilt complicates feminist rage—and slows down feminist activism. There is the mother's guilt toward her children, and the non-mother's guilt that she has evaded the central life dramas of intimacy and separation described so well in feminist writing about motherhood.

So, in conclusion, what? It's no part of my argument to say women shouldn't want children. This would be to trivialize the complexity of wishes, to call mothering a sort of false consciousness—a belittling suggestion. Women have incorporated a great deal into their mothering, but one question for feminism should surely be: Do we want this new capacious identity, mother, to expand or to contract? How special do we want mothering to be? My reading makes more obvious than ever that feminists completely disagree on this point—or rather that there are many feminisms, different particularly on this point. And here's another viper's nest: Do feminists want men to become mothers, too; that is, to have primary child care responsibilities?

Again, the feminist work on this point veers wildly, is murky. Women ask, for example, "Can men really nurture?" And behind that doubt, or that insult, hides out knowledge of what psychological power mothers have. Why give that up, we may well ask. This wave of feminism was a great outburst of indignation. I suspect that it's important to us to feel that men are no longer necessary, particularly since lots of men are gone before the baby is two. Insofar as patriarchy means the protective law of the father, patriarchy's over.

I find a great cynicism among us about ever getting men's help, or the state's. Because we have won so few tangible victories, women tend to adopt a sort of Mother Courage stance now—long-suffering, almost sometimes a parody of being tireless—though it occurs to me, finally, that this picture I'm painting is much too bleak. Other questions hint at a more volatile situation altogether. How do we feminists greet and interpret the fact that women are voting with their feet, marrying later, using contraception and abortion and having fewer children? Might there be some opportunities for feminism buried in these broad, demographic changes?

Under what banner are we going to fly our demands for mothers? I like best the gender-neutral constructions of this cohort of the brilliant feminist lawyers. Yet as they would be first to point out, gender-neutral demands—for parenting leaves, disability, gender-blind custody—have their short-term price. We give up something, a special privilege wound up in the culture-laden word "mother" that we will not instantly regain in the form of freedom and power. We're talking about a slow process of change. Giving up the exclusivity of motherhood is bound to feel to many like loss. Only a fool gives up something present for something intangible and speculative, Jack exchanging the cow for a couple of beans. But even if we can't yet imagine our passage from here to there, from control over motherhood to shared, socialized parenthood, couldn't we talk about it, structure demands? An epigram keeps forming in my mind: "Just because you can't have something doesn't mean you don't want it—or shouldn't fight for it."

Let me end with a cautionary analogy: in the nineteenth century, feminism's idée fixe was the vote. We won it, but it was hard to make it mean something larger, to make it into a source of public authority for women. In our wave, the idée fixe has been abortion. If we're lucky, and if we work very hard, we may win it. But there will be much resistance to letting the right to abortion expand to its larger potential meaning. We seem—this time around—to really want abortion. And this right carries within it the seed of new identities for women.

Carolyn Morell

On Needing and Finding Courage

Remaining childless takes guts. From my experience, if you are a woman who is not a mother, cultural messages will conspire to inform you of your incompleteness and your inadequacy and your inferior life. These messages can rob you of your comfortable nonconformity. If you let them.

I make a habit of collecting pro-mothering viewpoints that wound. Some of the statements entered in my journal are straightforward assaults on childless women. Consider the following:

5/20/87: Visit to Dr. G. to get my back aligned. He asked what my dissertation topic was—I told him intentionally childless women. Big mistake. He said in so many words childless women are: tense, very tense; prone to worry as they get older (don't like going out of their houses); become isolated as they age; nuns are especially tense; career women become too self-absorbed; it's an unnatural way to live. He makes it a game to "guess" about his female patients before he looks at their card. He can usually tell the childless ones.

For some reason I'm *vulnerable* to these kinds of beliefs. My fears are obviously involved here. Do his statements reflect reality or prejudice or both? Isn't it more a matter of "personality" than motherhood/nonmotherhood? There are tense mothers and nonmothers, calm mothers and nonmothers. Actually, most people are calm sometimes and tense sometimes, depending on circumstances. How important a category is this anyway?

I came home depressed by his comments. I received confirmation of the attitudes that exist out there in the real world. Will I be perceived as a dried up old prune because I am childless? I realize this is self-indulgent negative thinking, but these thoughts do cross my mind.

Sometimes the ideas about childlessness that upset me are delivered out of ignorance; sometimes from spite. Whatever the motivation, they have the power to sting and to confuse. Some of the disconcerting messages I've collected over the years are delivered in a backhanded way—they are designed not to make childless women feel bad but to make mothers feel good:

> Children make death more bearable. They are our future and their love helps to lessen the loneliness of dying.[1]

These sentences suggest that children are the only source of comfort, the prime necessity for a cozy death. Those without children are rendered invisible. Of course children may be a real emotional resource to parents. Those without children may have real emotional resources as well. They are different. Yet sources of support other than children are rarely acknowledged and legitimated.

Some cultural communications are intended to be "liberal," allowing reproductive difference. An example is a newspaper article I came across in 1987 titled, "Private Lives: Saying 'No' to Kids, Some Couples Find a Twosome is Quite Enough." If this article had appeared unadorned I might have found its message reassuring. But juxtaposed on the same page directly below the main article is the story of the woman who wrote the article. Her autobiographical statement is framed by a black border and printed on a background of light red ink. The headline reads: "For Her it was Love, Marriage, Family."

> Now that I know the insistent demands of babies and young children, the light hand needed in guiding teen-agers without stifling them, I understand why career couples hesitate to add a family to their lives . . . I also realize how naive—and blessed—we were in becoming parents and also how grateful I am that I don't have to struggle with the decision, which has turned out to be the most demanding—and rewarding—thing I've done with my life.[2]

So much for childlessness as a viable option. I ask you to imagine a human interest article about gays and lesbians that on the same page features a statement by the heterosexual author expounding on

---

[1] See Eda LeShan, *Oh, to Be 50 Again.* (New York: Pocket Books, 1988), p. 255.

[2] Paula Voell. "For Her It Was Love, Marriage, Family." In *The Buffalo News*, Sunday, April 12, 1987, p. 1F.

the glories of heterosexuality and expressing her gratitude for being a heterosexual.

To be childless is simultaneously to be reminded of your second-rate life and to be ignored. As I grew into my middle years I went to the popular and scholarly literatures about midlife for information and inspiration. What I found is that writers and researchers assume all adult women are mothers. The very definitions of midlife erase not-mothering women. Lillian Rubin, who wrote *Women of a Certain Age: The Midlife Search for Self*, defines midlife not as a stage tied to chronological age but as the post-parental years, "the point in the life cycle of the family when children are grown and gone, or nearly so."[3] And in *In Her Prime: A New View of Middle-aged Women*, anthropologist Judith K. Brown devises her own meaning: "Middle-aged women (matrons) are women who have adult offspring and who are not yet frail or dependent."[4] According to these definitions, I am not a middle-aged woman. I certainly am not a middle-aged man. My midlife crisis suffers a perverse twist.

Many of the predictable patterns that may fit the experience of mothers do not "fit" the life of a woman without children. For example, the common notion of an "empty nest" has no application to the lives of childless women. Do those of us without children never or always experience this problem? In fact the characteristics and impact of the "nest" are different for women without children and we lack a literature to characterize that difference. The experiences of not-mothering women have yet to be named. Our lives remain untheorized.

More accurately, our lives are under- and wrongly theorized. When we are studied, we are often pathologized even by those highly respected in the academic world:

> Feminists like to point up the psychic costs for women of
> marriage and motherhood; but whereas the childless woman
> can never have a post-partum psychosis, being maternal may

---

[3]Lillian B. Rubin, *Women of a Certain Age: The Midlife Search for Self.* (New York: Harper and Row, Publishers, 1979), p. 7.

[4]Judith K. Brown, V. Kerns, et. al. *In Her Prime: A New View of Middle-Aged Women.* (South Hadley, Massachusetts: Bergin & Garvey Publishers, 1985), p. 2.

protect women—perhaps even narcissistic women—against the psychoses of *later* life.[5]

The authors of the above statement divide a psychiatric population of childless women into two categories, "aging tomboys" and "perpetual daughters." They perceive all childless women as remaining "disastrously vulnerable to the later life intimations of mortality" since they have never experienced "that great transformation of narcissim that renders the child's life more precious than their own." Biological motherhood is so pivotal that those who resist are likely to become "developmental casualties." DEVELOPMENTAL CASUALTY. Remaining childless is an ongoing test of perseverance.

So I turn to the feminist movement, a source of support throughout my adult life. Do I find validation and a friendlier construction of childlessness? My need for courage only increases. The strong public feminist voice of the early 1970s, arguing that women could have good lives without motherhood, is barely audible today. A maternal revivalism has occured over the past two decades within feminism as well as in the dominant culture. As I read my books, journals and newspapers, they suggest that motherhood is not only an okay choice for women but the absolutely wonderful choice. Indeed it is motherhood which turns women into morally superior beings:

9/14/83: (After a Women's Studies class:)
I'm having very strong feelings about a baby right now. Can you believe this?! Just a few minutes ago in class K. (the professor) asked us, "Do you think that women are peacemakers because of the experience of having children?" And again, "Are women against war because they don't want their children hurt?" *Hey, I'm against war and I don't have children!!!* I feel invisible when I hear things like this—that motherhood turns women into saints. Maybe I should think about pregnancy? I can't believe this!

I can see in this journal entry that doubts about being childless and thoughts about giving up the practice usually arise in the context of feeling tired of being different. I just want to get this "difference" over with. I want to be a regular woman.

---

[5]See David Gutman, J. Grunes, and B. Griffin, "The Clinical Psychology of Later Life: Developmental Paradigms." In Nancy Datan and N. Lohmann, eds., *Transitions of Aging.* (New York: Academic Press, 1980), pp. 119-131.

During this contemporary period of feminism, the do-both ideology is strong: Have a dazzling career but be a mother too.

That women should have babies rather than books is the considered opinion of Western Civilization. That women should have books rather than babies is a variation on the theme.[6]

In this scenario, the suggestion is that all women should be mothers whatever else they do. Here I am consigned to a half-life of my own doing.

These selected quotations point to an entrenched condition: remaining childless does not share equal status and privilege with the decision (or nondecision) to mother. As Ann Ferguson points out, motherhood may be financially detrimental but in a pronatalist culture mothers have the dominant ideology on their side. Being a mother has psychological advantages.[7]

Although childless women share a common context we do not all react to this context in the same way. For some women cultural messages hold little power. As one woman I interviewed put it, "You have to understand, Carolyn—childlessness—it's just not in my head." That is not my experience. I take pronatalism personally. For me, sensitivity to popular meanings of childlessness requires negotiation.

To gain courage I talk to myself. I repeat the wise words of others too numerous to mention. I say to myself: Don't listen to these cultural voices. Resist reproducing their message. *There is nothing helpful there.*[8] Instead, I practice tenderness towards and determination about my difference. I see myself as a participant in the historical struggle of women to live their lives beyond society's dictates and strictures. I see myself as a woman who defies the moral order despite ideological sanction.

---

[6]See Alicia Ostriker, *Writing Like A Woman*. (Ann Arbor, University of Michigan Press, 1983).

[7]See Ann Ferguson, *Blood at the Root: Motherhood, Sexuality and Male Dominance*. (London: Pandora, 1989).

[8]I lifted this sentence from Natalie Goldberg's essay called "Doubt is Torture." It fits what I want to say. I also use some of her ideas and phrases. Thank you Natalie. See *Writing Down the Bones: Freeing the Writer Within*.π (Boston & London, Shambhala, 1986), p. 108-9.

I listen to voices that empower. For instance, Bell Hooks proposes that marginalization not only signifies deprivation, it creates an opportunity to construct oneself anew.[9] When I remember this my balance returns. I feel like a pioneer practicing one essential version of reproductive choice.

An equally important way I sustain myself is through careful investigation of my lived experience rather than acceptance of the dominant cultural construction of my experience. Closely observed, my life lacks nothing. I have what I need to be happy, everything a woman could need. I have my body, my consciousness, my life. I have strong loving bonds with family members and friends of diverse ages, and meaningful relationships with other species. I have important work that I care about. I have material comforts and resources. Indeed, my life is enormously privileged compared to that of most people on the planet. My actual experience satisfies—it is the cultural concept of childlessness that creates doubt or fear.

The identity offered to childless women, despite some historical fluctuations, remains a deficient one. This symbolic degradation can create discomfort and pressure to conform. Yet the disadvantage also establishes an opening for developing a realistic and comfortable sense of self that is not so tied to cultural norms.

My experience as a childless woman reminds me of the great diversity among women. And it also reinforces my understanding of our common needs. While respecting and supporting our differences we can move together toward collective goals, such as the establishment of conditions that allow for full reproductive freedom. In the world we create, women will mother without penalty and remain childless without censure.

---

[9]See Bell Hooks, *Yearning: Race, Gender, and Cultural Politics.* (Boston: South End Press, 1990).

Eloise Klein Healy

Artemis

I am thinking about romance and its purpose.
Children and why I didn't have any.
I would have left the cave and them with it
or I would have tied them to me forever
with my own sad dreams and finicky order.

I've liked young animals better.
I could put their heads in my mouth.
I could lick and clean them like a mother,
but I could not raise a child.
The first thing a child should see
is the pink sunrise of a nipple, not the green wind
of a branch whipping in passing.

I chose to keep animals around me instead
because we are the same. We have habits
and make strange circles before we sleep.
We don't like to be watched while we eat.

Elissa A. Raffa

The Vow

I remember the day I decided to never have children. It is in the spring of sixth grade, the end of my second year in public school, and Mrs. Dolan is nothing like any nun or lay teacher I've ever had. She has broad shoulders, and wiry black hair that leaps from her high forehead. She uses the daily newspaper as a text for our reading and writing lessons, and she listens to us students like our lives are worth something.

Mrs. Dolan never tells me I'm wrong about anything. She's the kind of woman I want to grow up to be: solid and smart and apparently not attached to a man. She never talks about her husband, and it takes me to April of that school year, when she finally drops some mention of him, to figure out that she is married. I am heartbroken, but I scold myself about how I should have known what 'Mrs.' meant. Still, she hasn't mentioned any children. That, in itself, is interesting.

It is the end of a long, hot, uneventful Friday, just minutes before the bell will send us spilling out to the line of yellow buses. The buses wait with their motors idling. The exhaust drifts in the open window. Mrs. Dolan sits in her usual place on the front edge of her desk, where she can be closer to her students. Her green cotton skirt is hiked up a little, and I can almost reach out from my first row seat to touch her knee, which is covered in nylon. I am too sleepy to listen well, so I close my ears and watch the words form on her lips. Suddenly, some part of my brain wakes me up to the urgency of what she is saying.

"People who were abused as children grow up to abuse their own children." She holds a clipping from the *New York Times*, a report on the results of a sociological study.

Maybe Mrs. Dolan hasn't noticed the black-and-blue bruises that peek out from the cuff of my short-sleeved madras shirt. Maybe she isn't talking directly to me. Still, the knowledge rings through my body: *I am never having children.* I look around to make sure I haven't spoken this vow out loud.

It isn't a new thought. It is the confirmation of a danger I have always felt, a kind of dread that tightens in my twelve-year-old chest at the sight of infants in strollers. I begrudge them their neediness. I do not want anyone dependent on me, for food or anything else. I always thought this made me selfish.

Of all the adult women in my family, on both my mother's and father's side, only one, my Aunt Bea, has no children. It is not that

Aunt Bea *doesn't* have children, it is that she *can't*. It is a tragedy, not a choice. It is 1971 and I have never heard of abortion, yet my impulse is to refuse motherhood. Mrs. Dolan's words help me to see this impulse in a righteous light: not having children will be my contribution to lessening the injustice in the world.

Mrs. Dolan puts the clipping down on the desk. She doesn't ask the class, like she usually does, for questions or comments. We sit in terrible silence until the bell rings. "Have a good weekend," she says, as if nothing has changed. But I have made a vow.

A week later, my first period comes while I am wearing white shorts and playing after school at Marcy Goldberg's house. Marcy's basement is outfitted as her very own art studio. We are making horses out of modeling clay when I feel the sticky warmth spreading through my shorts.

"I have to go," I tell Marcy. She wants to know if she should bake my horse in the kiln, but I am up the stairs and out into the blasting afternoon sun. I run the quarter mile home, strip off my blood-stained shorts, and help myself to a Modess pad and elastic belt from the box my sisters keep in the hall closet.

It is unusual that no one is home. My sister Angela, back from college for the summer, has taken my mother out shopping. I pace the house, trying to adjust to the strange lump between my legs. My mother and sister come in with shopping bags, and lay out their purchases on my mother's bed. I watch them from the doorway to her room.

"I got my period," I announce.

My mother asks, "How did you know about that," as if the fact that she has never bothered to tell me anything could stem the tide of my sexual development.

I run into the bathroom and slam the door. I open it and slam it, open it and slam it, so that the mirrors rattle on the wall. I hate my mother. I hate her.

"Open up," Angela says.

I open the door a crack. She pushes her way in, and slams the door behind her. Then she hoists herself onto the long pink Formica counter and grabs hold of my shoulders.

"Don't listen to Mommy," she says. "She's crazy. She's too freaked out to talk about body stuff. Let me help."

My sister shows me how to rinse my white shorts in cold water. She gives me her own copy of *Our Bodies, Ourselves*. She intends for me to read the chapters on pregnancy and birth control, but every night in bed, before I fall asleep, I read the chapter, "In Amerika They

Call Us Dykes." My mother and I never discuss my period again. She never tells me that now I can be a mother. She has borne four daughters, and it is not a job she would recommend.

This is my body. The words from the Mass become my mantra. They separate me from the blows that fall on me, and from the huge man named Daddy who delivers the blows. *This is my body. Mine.* At six, I improvise a hunger strike. For days, maybe weeks, I refuse to eat anything but white grapes and Saltine crackers. My father's fury grows, but I have found new power: I can control what goes into my body. *This is my body, not his. And I am never having children.*

My mother is sick with Multiple Sclerosis, and I am the youngest daughter. At fourteen, I am old enough to cook and clean, but not old enough to escape like my sisters did to college, a job, or an efficiency apartment. Every afternoon, I come straight home from school so my mother won't be alone when her attendant leaves at 2:00. Every night I cook for my parents: *rigatoni* with meatballs, or meatloaf, or *pasta e fagioli.* Always a mixed green salad with oil and vinegar. Everything seasoned with a large dose of resentment.

I think my mother should be cooking. Not because I am an ungrateful troublemaker as my father would have it, but because she can. I want her to stay engaged, to hold on to the abilities she has, to fight isolation and not give up. But she has my father talking in her other ear, telling her that she is already useless. He orders her physical therapist and occupational therapist out of our house, even though insurance will pay for their weekly visits. He doesn't want these women, these strangers, meddling in how he runs his home.

My mother is depressed as well as disabled. She has withdrawn from her life; she has no opinions about anything, not even what she eats or watches on TV. I set two ultimatums: First, I will cook, but I will not think about what to cook. She will have to create the menus. Second, I am a vegetarian. I will cook meat but I will not sit down with them and eat it. I exaggerate my role as a servant, putting dinner on the table, and then retreating into my bedroom with a cheese sandwich. On nights when my father works late, I eat my cheese sandwich at the table with my mother, and leave his dinner in covered pots on the stove.

On nights that he is home, when I slam his plate down in front of him, my father says, "You'll make somebody a good wife some day."

"I'm not getting married." My answer never varies.

"Sure you will, some day, after college."

"Never," I contradict him. "I'm never getting married."

21

"Don't say that." He frowns sadly. "A woman needs to get married and have children." His beliefs are not so different from other Italian men, but he speaks with the added authority of his medical school training. "A woman is not a woman until she has brought forth a child from her womb. It is a woman's highest duty to bear children. It is her biological function. That is why she has a uterus."

"What is *your* biological function?" I ask him. "To get women pregnant?"

My mother begs me to stop talking like that. So disrespectful. But I know his answer. His highest duty is to use his superior brain. Mine is to pass his superior intellect on to a male child.

I want to use my own brain. I want to think and write, talk and laugh, and argue about politics. I want to be generous and have many friends. But I want no one to need me: no husband or child or parent. I fantasize about living alone in a small house at the edge of a small town. There are fields and woods nearby, and I can write at home and walk every day to the post office. I imagine living with dogs and cats, and many friends coming and going at all hours of the day and night. But I can always say good-bye, lock the door and be alone.

At thirty-three, my life in Minneapolis fits fairly well with my teenage fantasy. My little white house looks like a farmhouse, in spite of the cheap asbestos siding. I live alone on the first floor; a friend rents the apartment upstairs. We don't live in the country, but the kitchen is outfitted with 1940s farmhouse appliances and the empty lot next door has become a community garden for several of the neighbors on the block. I can walk to the post office, to a beautiful urban park, to my lover's house, or to visit several of my friends. In the morning, I go to work as a teacher; in the evening, I do my writing at home. Many people do come and go, and many political meetings happen around my kitchen table. I am happy to cook *rigatoni* with mushroom sauce for my friends; to welcome my lover into my bed; to say good-bye, lock the door and be alone sometimes. I am happy that no one—not even a dog or a cat—depends on me for dinner every night. Most of the time, I do a good job of watering the plants.

Once every year or two, on my visits to New York, my father corners me with unsound, unsolicited medical advice.

"Get your hormones rebalanced," he tells me. "You don't have to be a lesbian forever."

"You don't know what the fuck you're talking about." I yell at him for my own sake but also for the sake of the lesbian patients he might have burdened with such a suggestion. Has he actually *prescribed* hormone treatments as a cure for lesbianism? I am too afraid to ask.

When he sees I mean business, he changes his tune. "You should look into artificial insemination," he says. "You don't have to be childless forever." In his book, it is worse for a woman to have no children than to raise children without a father.

Since the early 1980s, I have witnessed every possible method of lesbians achieving pregnancy: with frozen and fresh sperm, from known and unknown donors, delivered by doctors, midwives, friends who are go-betweens, or sometimes delivered by the donor himself, in an artichoke jar or even by fucking. I sat in on the early discussions about lesbians seizing our reproductive capacity as a revolutionary act, and on more recent discussions about lesbian motherhood as an anti-revolutionary waste of time. I have watched lesbians who have been out to their parents for ten or fifteen years agonize over how to break the news that now they are pregnant.

Even my friend Barbara, whose parents are pro-choice activists, must prepare herself for a fight: a child needs a father; how can you choose to burden a child like this; you're being selfish; you can't have it both ways. After a while her parents will adjust to the idea, come to visit, and bounce a happy grandson on their knee.

No one but me has a father who actually pushes artificial insemination. "Many single women are choosing AI," he instructs me.

"I'm sure they are, but I'm not interested in motherhood. And it's my uterus." *Mine.*

"Of course it's your uterus. Who said it wasn't?"

"I'm saying it's none of your business how I use it."

I never tell him that I have already offered to have AI and give the baby to my sister Angela.

It's a deal that never comes through, but it is one I am willing to make out of love for my sister. Angela had cancer when she was twenty-eight, a vaginal tumor caused by my mother taking DES while she was pregnant, and all the radiation and surgery has messed up her reproductive system.

At twenty-three, I fly to New York for my grandmother's ninety-fifth birthday party.

"Come here," Angela says and pulls me into the bathroom, still our refuge in our parents' house. We used to spend hours together in this salmon-tiled room, her comforting me when I cried, or me hanging out to watch her straighten her hair around beer can curlers and put on white eye shadow to get ready for dates with teenage boys.

Her hair and eye make-up are fine; she has dragged me in here to proposition me.

She wants kids really bad and she's checking out her options. She doesn't want to bullshit about her ability to raise a kid of color; she wants a white kid, and adoptions take forever. She's looking into direct adoption, and she's approaching both me and a cousin who already has kids about having a baby for her. Would I?

"Sure," I say on the spur of the moment. Although I have never wanted to raise a child, I realize that my first response to the idea of being pregnant is pretty neutral. I do feel squeamish at the thought of her husband Ron being the sperm donor, and at her whole emphasis on getting the baby to be as genetically similar as possible to the two of them. I don't challenge her on the white baby issue: at least she can admit what a cultural vacuum she lives in. This is before Baby M and the media debates about surrogacy. We don't talk details. We don't talk about what if I went through the pregnancy and couldn't bear to part with the child, probably because neither of us can imagine me acting that way. We also don't talk about how we will tell the child. Or what if we differ about *whether* to tell the child.

That conversation is the closest I ever come to getting pregnant. Within a few months, Angela and Ron have arranged a direct adoption. They have a daughter, and I am off the hook.

Which doesn't mean that my uterus ceases to be a topic of conversation. I visit New York less and less frequently, but I hear reports from my old best friend, Jacob.

Jacob and I were inseparable all through junior high and high school and since I have moved away, his social life revolves around two of my sisters. He's Jewish, always available on Catholic holidays, and always invited to holiday dinners at my parents' house. My mother's fifth daughter, we call him. Or, my replacement.

Everyone knows that Jacob is gay, everyone acts like they've never heard of HIV, and they all have him picked out as my sperm donor.

"You should have heard it," he tells me after Easter dinner one year. "Your father, your sisters. They're all telling me how you should have a baby and how I should provide the sperm."

As my sisters get older, they have become curious about my reproductive capacity. It is something they wouldn't think twice about if theirs were working well. But all three of them have struggled with different reproductive health problems and I, being the youngest, am the most likely to have escaped the damaging effects of DES. My mother's obstetrician closed his office years ago and shredded the

24

files. We can't prove that she didn't take the drug while she carried me. But everyone is assuming that I could get pregnant on the first try. They imagine that I am letting a precious resource go to waste.

I don't tell Jacob that they're probably wrong. While he was out learning about gay sex, and before I even knew how to find lesbians, I was learning about hetero sex in the cramped back seats of cars. Three or four times a week for all of eleventh grade I took the risk of fucking with no birth control, and although I worried a lot, I never got pregnant.

I ask Jacob to quit repeating my family's comments to me. "I purposely don't visit," I remind him. "So why should I want to hear their crap through you? Besides, did you tell them your sperm is promised elsewhere?"

It is promised to Barbara, my best friend in Minneapolis.

"He's cute," she whispers the first time she meets him. "And Jewish. Do you think he would be a sperm donor?"

"Ask him," I encourage her.

The weather is sweltering—Jacob picked the hottest two weeks of summer to visit—so we seek relief by going to the longest movies we can find. We watch *Fannie and Alexander* and *Ghandi* in air conditioned comfort, in the middle of the day when they're cheap.

When we run out of movies, we hang out at the Science Museum in the hands-on technology exhibit. We play with the robot arm, and the whisper dishes—two parabolic reflectors that make it possible to hear someone speaking in hushed tones from all the way across the museum.

It is in the whisper dishes that Barbara propositions Jacob. He says he'll think about it.

The next time she sees him is three years later, when he visits Minneapolis again. Barbara has a lover, a house, a job. She is ready to have a baby.

"Do you think he's still willing," she wants to know.

"Ask him," I say.

He is willing, even to be HIV tested—something he was opposed to before on political grounds. They get together to talk schedules and contracts. She'll buy him an airline ticket back here for the two or three days around her next ovulation. He'll be unemployed and free to travel by then. They negotiate his level of involvement: how many visits per year, how long each visit can be.

I think maybe I have made a mistake. What if Jacob takes Barbara to court for custody and it's my fault for introducing them? Not likely. I know these friends; I know they can both be counted on.

Then what if I change my mind about not having children? Maybe *I* should be negotiating these things with Jacob.

It isn't that I want children, it's just that every once in a while I reconsider my vow. In the years since I left my parent's house, I have learned to stop panicking at the sight of infants. I have learned to hold them close to my chest, instead of at arm's length; to appreciate their helplessness and how they change by leaps and bounds; to believe that it is possible to interpret and to satisfy their needs. I have gone from saying never to probably not to maybe. After all, this is my body. My choice. Will I ever decide yes? Probably not.

What would have to be true before you would be ready to have a baby—or another baby, if you are already a mother? It is a writing assignment I give my high school women's studies class every year. Some of my students are mothers; some already have their second child. Most of them are thousands of times more likely to get pregnant than I am. Still, I always do the assignment.

I would have to be willing to spend one third of my income on daycare. I would have to be willing to raise a son. I would have to be willing to put my writing, political activism, and other commitments on hold for a few years. I would have to change my habit of doing a million things in one day from six a.m. to midnight. I would lose the freedom to say yes to anything that comes my way. At thirty-one, I amend my vow.

I vow never to have children, not out of fear, but in freedom. I have enough time to be a good auntie to my friends' children, and to my sister's—although it is harder from a distance of 1200 miles. I have enough time to offer my phone as the referral number for a Young Lesbians and Friends group, to take calls from sixteen and seventeen-year-old women who have never talked to a "gay woman" before. I have enough time to use my brain and my big mouth, to make trouble at my job, in local politics, wherever I can. I have a spare room in my house, which I can offer to friends in crisis who need a temporary place to stay. And enough money to keep the room empty and unheated when the crisis is past and I really want to be alone.

"You'll be lonely when you're old," my father warns me, "if you don't have children."

He is frail now, and fifty pounds thinner since a stroke ripped through his left side. His thick black hair has all turned to white. He is still cruel to my mother, but I refrain from being cruel to him. I don't say: *Look at you. You had four children, and not one of us will be taking care of you.* But it is true. We all do our best to avoid him.

As far as I know, he has never had a friend in his life, except maybe the man who owned the Italian pastry shop around the corner from his office. Except for his daily cup of *espresso* with the other old men there, I never saw him socialize with anyone. Except for his accountant and lawyer, he never invited anyone to our house. When he was *my* age, a young father, he was lonely. But he worries about *me* being a barren old maid.

"Listen," I tell him. "I'm never having children. And that's not the end of what's interesting about my life; it's the beginning."

He never asks me what I mean.

Stephanie Harris

Ecce Ancilla Domini (Dante Gabriel Rossetti, 1850)

You've got the oval face and flowing hair
that Rossetti would have loved:
he'd have painted you, then seduced you,
then painted you again and again,

as Mary in his depiction of the Annunciation,
shrinking against her bedroom wall while the archangel Gabriel
stands pointing the stem of a lily
directly towards her womb.

You, like Mary, were ambivalent about the whole idea
but as the inevitable unfolded, the rhythm of a second beat
beneath your own worked its magic on you until
you awaited it eagerly, were made to wait even longer,
and suffer in childbirth, another valediction,
in case you'd missed the point.

And afterwards, how we all gathered around to see
and touch your child, to stroke her tiny head
or hold her for just a moment.

I, in my narrow hard bed and white nightgown,
would shrink from such a coming, if it were I,
would dread the weight of inexorable glory,
the weight of a pregnancy,

wishing for something splendid to happen to me
but resenting the form it might take:
to be nothing more than a fruit that bears seeds,

mere receptacle for a miraculous birth,
never the miracle itself.

Nina Silver

The Abortion

"You had *what?*"

My mother's bulgy eyed
     mouth in a line
wearing incomprehension like a jacket

cold wind clattering

Meanwhile I stand
still,
     steady
     fighting the wall
flushed-out uterus
heaving
     swollen
     sore
     swaddled in separation

"It must have been a *goyishe* fetus.
You gave it up because
     the man wasn't Jewish."

I lean and laugh,
     a teary protest

There was no room in my life
for another
     no matter how beautiful
you see, Ma
I am just beginning
     to awaken
          to daybreak
          to joy
to my own childlike laugh
the one you can't take away
     no matter
     how much you scowl

Alison Solomon

An Empty Womb

I have never seen a poem
about the ugliness of periods.
Periods (apparently) are miraculous.
Moon-cycles regulating our lives
beauty reminiscent of blood-red flowers.
They are womanliness
Power
A bond with nature.

I have never seen a poem
describing the anxious wait
hoping not to find, but finding
blood.
Again.
Knowing that periods
are not miraculous.
The deep red flowers are merely proof
of an empty womb.

I have never seen a poem
suggesting
that periods are a state of mind.
That even an empty womb
is beautiful.

When I see these poems
I will know that
infertile women write poetry too.

Randi Locke

Choosing Childlessness

When my husband and I reached the agonizing decision not to have a baby, we were accused of being a multitude of things—including selfish, immature, irresponsible, thoughtless, heartless, cheap, and heading for the biggest mistake of our lives.

The sexes reacted differently to our decision. Our women friends were much more judgmental than the men, who, for the most part, remained mute but amused that my husband actually "scored points on this one." The women either sputtered angrily—"I would demand it!" and "Make it an ultimatum!" were typical comments—or expressed bewilderment. Why would a healthy, intelligent, working but not career-driven woman be an accomplice to this monumentally self-destructive decision? They dismissed it as an unfortunate case of brainwashing on my husband's part.

I understood exactly how they felt. Born smack in the middle of the baby boom, I was a stereotypical product of my generation, growing up in a close and happy family. The imperative to "go forth and multiply" was inherent in my Jewish upbringing. My husband, Neil, also empathized with this consensus. After all, he reasoned, he was a parent from his first marriage, and his daughter most probably would have had at least one other sibling had that marriage survived.

Nevertheless, we believed that this extremely personal and very painful decision was the absolute best one given our circumstances.

Those circumstances, however, don't seem to be acceptable excuses for not procreating among our peer group. Most happily-married couples decide against children for a number of "legitimate" reasons: genetic disease, health, infertility, personal philosophy, finances—none of which apply to us. Our chromosomes are in good shape, our health in fine form, our ability to conceive a-okay (which was proved during one highly distressing period in our lives when the abortion issue struck a personal chord). And despite our fling with 1960s values, we are not hard-core pessimists leery of bringing a child into this devastated world.

For my husband, having a baby boiled down to a question of simple economics. We need two incomes to survive the mortgage. A baby would eliminate one income, at least for a time, jeopardizing our equity. That reasoning appeared to falter, however, when people suggested that we start a new life in a less expensive region of the country. And this logic was reduced to mere rhetoric when we would fantasize about what we would do with more money, and having a baby was nowhere to be found on his wish list.

Still, what our friends really couldn't fathom was that I do not have the genuine maternal instincts that cause other females to issue rash ultimata to their resistant mates. In spite of (or perhaps because of) my nurtured and affectionate upbringing, inflated sensitivity, and profound desire to heal others less fortunate than me, I do not seem to possess the instinctual drive to make babies. Whatever it is that tugs at the heartstrings, that plays havoc with a woman's conscience, that drives all the other priorities in her life to the bottom of the list, is authentically absent in me.

At the outset, I didn't deliberately decide against children. The decision developed gradually. Like the millions of other boomers who started "growing up" late, I envisioned motherhood in the abstract, as an inevitable phase that would eventually catch up to me when the climate was right. Being the over-protected "baby" in the family, (with only one sibling, a sister eight years my senior who magically disappeared from family life between meals), I was rarely, if ever, exposed to babies.

I was certain, though, that despite my lack of experience, obsessive fear of physical pain, and procrastinating nature, my husband and I would have children, thus joining the ranks of millions of other "normal" Americans. In fact, prior to our marriage, we spoke at great length about it and not only to ourselves. Neil made it a point to speak out each time his willingness was questioned. He convinced everyone, including me, that he was committed to providing me with everything "essential" to a young, married woman's life—that he would never dream of "depriving" me of what I "so rightfully deserved." But this verbal pledge started wearing thin as the years progressed and his deeds didn't live up to his words.

I had questioned my own allegiance to parenthood over and over again in my head, noting the ambivalence, the continuous postponing, the discussions with Neil that evolved into heated debates—and finally determined that in order for us to start a family, I would require nothing short of a complete emotional commitment from my husband. It would be unacceptable to witness him going through the motions of being "Mr. Mom" without the necessary accommodating feelings. He would have to want this child absolutely as much as I . . . perhaps even more. In view of my apprehension, I needed to be coaxed. I needed a partner who would insist on a family, who would take me by the hand and, in essence, give me that extra push. And although his shaky voice would try to reassure me, I knew better. While I saw compassion in his good intentions, I knew the desire for a child wasn't in his heart. So I decided, finally, to let it go. The stress and tension that babies are capable of creating were not worth it to me. The final proof of that growing conviction was when I consented to my husband's vasectomy.

I would be lying if I said that it doesn't hurt when I see the baby boomlet erupting before my eyes. Women (and men) with infants and children have managed to haunt every aspect of my life. From shopping centers to parks to beaches to restaurants to movie theaters (in the audience and on the screen), children are center-stage everywhere, all the time. Family occasions, neighborly barbecues, weddings, surprise parties, casual get togethers, my office (is nothing sacred?) . . . there's no escaping the reality. The mindless chatter that accompanies this new surge in population gnaws at me each time I'm exposed. Perhaps I'm intensely disturbed over the issue, but it seems that virtually everyone is obsessed with "baby" these days.

If the proud parents (or grandparents) are not boasting about their pint-sized wonders, then they're bubbling over expecting one. When you're childless, there's only one thing more uncomfortable than little people running around in clothes more expensive than your own, and that is seeing beaming, bulging, pregnant women and their spouses, one hand cupping the baby-to-be.

I realize Freudians would have a field day with my psyche, insisting that I am terribly resentful, that I have repressed my significant feelings and probably hunger for a thumb-sucking tyke to call my own. Perhaps. Still, my husband and I cannot be the only couple sharing this dilemma.

In this era of self-help, with hundreds of support groups springing up to accommodate every problem under the sun, it would be safe to assume that one must exist for childless couples. Wrong. The truth of the matter is that there seems to be no group that meets our needs. After contacting a number of agencies and referral services in my area (Long Island), I have received either blank stares, shrugs or gratuitous referrals to fertility centers. Countless times I would find myself explaining that we are searching for couples who have consciously decided against having children. Frosty the Snowman would have been capable of a warmer reception than the ones I've received from some of these "sympathetic" bureaucrats.

Baffled market researchers are exasperated because today's demographics are so astounding. Gays and lesbians have gained greater acceptance and are asserting their rights as parents; single women are having babies solo; women old enough to be young grandmas are giving birth for the first time; men over 60 are recreating the fatherly role they once believed was behind them forever; mentally

33

retarded people are growing more independent and are marrying and starting families; children with children are carrying school books in one arm, their baby in the other. All of these groups seem to find the necessary support. But the consciously childless couple is an unrecognized enigma.

Despite the impressive numbers (four out of 10 married couples in the US do not have children), my husband and I feel extremely isolated. Most of these couples will have children eventually and the ones that don't either can't—or won't. The ones that won't are most likely engrossed in fast track careers that consume most of their time and energies. Those in our position, wherever they are, are very much alone . . . and most likely lonely.

The stigma of being childless in today's society is more painful than most people will admit, especially now that we are entering the "traditional '90s." I am well aware of the negative repercussions. In fact, during my darker moments I fear that someday I might "wake up" to regret my decision. While most readers are undoubtedly shaking their heads, thinking my anticipated remorse is inevitable, I have accepted the fact that, for me, having children was never meant to be. I'm proud, too, that I have dared to demonstrate what the feminist movement has simply uttered—that not all women are meant to be mothers.

Michele Patenaude

On Not Having Children

My mother knows I don't want to have any children. If she has a problem with that, she doesn't let on. Perhaps it doesn't matter to her; my two older sisters have made her a grandmother four times over.

I am just one of the four children my mother raised. She says we were all wanted. I certainly appreciate the sentiment, thought I'm not sure I believe her. She doesn't say we were all *planned*. That I wouldn't believe.

Planning implies decision, and decision, choice. And for a woman of my mother's generation and class, childbearing was not a choice. (Unless you consider lifelong virginity a choice.)

The last of us, my brother, was four years old when the FDA approved The Pill. Too late for mom, but plenty of time for me, only six years old.

I was already "on" the pill two years and about to celebrate my 19th birthday, when the Supreme Court decided *Roe vs. Wade*. I often thank my lucky stars I was not born sooner, by even a decade. I am in the first generation of women for whom having children is an option, not a sentence. My mom and I, one generation apart, a biological revolution between us.

I was in my mid-twenties when I first realized that I didn't want to have children. Like so many other milestones in my baby-boomer life, I assumed I would be joined in that decision by a tidal wave of female peers. I thought that, having been given reproductive emancipation, few of us would choose to be enslaved by motherhood.

An ill-conceived prediction

I envisioned an America that would soon reach zero population growth, then less-than-zero. Sometime around the year 2000, the government, in order to boost sagging birth rates, would start programs to entice women into bearing children—money, rewards, favors, preferences, free trips to Hawaii.

But even this would not be enough to lure women into 18 years of servitude to Gerber masters, Fischer-Price tyrants. The government would go beyond inducement to coercion and, eventually, enforcement. Abortion would be the first to go. Then there would be a ban on birth control. Women would be strapped to tables and artificially inseminated against their wills.

I was wrong.

At 33, I find all my over-30 friends are already pregnant mothers, clients at fertility clinics or nervously watching their fertile sands-of-time run out, while wondering if they should wait for the right man or take on parenthood solo. Am I the only one who looks forward to menopause?

Was it only ten years ago that we hung out in the kitchen at parties and compared notes on pills and loops and coils and copper Ts and foam and diaphragms and abortions? Now the talk is of children, pregnancy, natural childbirth, breastfeeding, sperm counts, blocked fallopian tubes, misfiring ovaries, artificial insemination, in-vitro fertilization, adoption, fertility pills, surrogacy contracts, baby-selling and baby-snatching.

I have nothing to say. I just listen to the deafening roar of our combined biological clocks *tick-tocking* away.

Mostly Mothers

Statistics tell me that one in seven of us are not biological clock watchers. We do not want children. Still, an overwhelming 85 percent do.

And most want two, a boy and a girl, in that order. My generation wanted to do its own thing but ended up doing the usual thing. That most of the women of my generation have so easily and willingly taken a course so permanent, so unalterable and so encompassing, astounds me.

Some believe in maternal instinct; a little voice we women are born with that whispers in our ears, "Have a baby. Have a baby. Have another baby." Some believe an estrogenic urge compels women to want to cuddle and nurture and coo and play peek-a-boo.

I don't believe in maternal instinct. If we, as women, have any instinct, it is to give ourselves up. To limit ourselves. To distract ourselves with taking care of others. To nurture everyone but ourselves.

We have babies not out of instinct but because we've been told from Day One and in a million little ways that having babies is normal, desirable, and good, from the dolls that are put in our cribs to the flowers we receive in the maternity ward. As women, we are creators of life. Motherhood, we are told, is the ultimate experience in a woman's life. A mystical experience. Female nirvana. Who can resist such a promise?

Gone to mothers one by one

I watched my friends and sisters have babies one by one. And with these babies went much of their freedom and most of their free time. I saw their marriages go from partnerships to roles. I saw women put their hobbies on hold, their vacations on hold, careers on hold, nights out with their friends on hold, themselves on hold.

Mothering has so much to recommend against it: morning sickness, labor pains, pushing strollers through crowded stores, 2 a.m. feedings, dirty diapers (I've heard that men are able to change diapers, but I've never actually seen it done), the putting on and taking off of snowsuits, teething, baby-sitters, standing in line to see Santa Claus, daycare, orthodonture, teenage boyfriends who drive loud cars with Playboy logo air fresheners hanging from rear view mirrors, college tuition, expensive weddings, difficult sons- and daughters-in-law.

I can hear my friends who are mothers, *tsk-tsk*ing me right now. Having children is not all work and problems, they tell me. I know they are right.

My friend's four-year-old brings her crumpled dandelions and says, "Mommy, I love you." A few years later she brings home straight-A report cards and wins the spelling bee. Her face on Christmas morning as she sees her new two-wheel bike will illuminate the day. I'm sure there are thousands of other incidents, words and memories that bring joy and fulfillment.

But right now there are too many books I want to read, to write. Too many hours of quiet and alone I want to have. Too many long walks. Too many Sunday mornings to be spent in bed. Too many hours watching birds and sunsets, the waves rolling in on a rocky beach. Too many options I'd prefer to leave open. Too many sacrifices I'd rather not make.

Selfish. Once I was told that I was, for having this view, for making this choice not to have children. But selfish seems such an inappropriate accusation to aim at a woman for not wanting a *hypothetical child*. From where I stand, having children by choice seems more selfish.

What the world needs now . . .

In a world that can no longer provide for those already born, the last thing needed is another child to add to the already-born five billion. What Mother Earth needs, I tell myself, is more women like me who do not want to be mothers. More women to put a stop to the need for more houses, food, water, gasoline, cities, jails, medicine,

TVs. I self-righteously comfort myself with the idea that childlessness is environmentally altruistic.

I find myself apologizing for my decision. I follow up my "I do not want to have any children," with "It's not that I don't like children. I do, but . . ." And I explain that I do not want to be a mother just as I do not want to be a doctor or an engineer or a farmer or a poet or an actor. Just as I do not want to climb Mount Everest, collect antiques or raise orchids.

Still, I'm ambivalent. I wonder if when I'm seventy, I'll look back to regret my choice. Secretly, I sometimes worry that I will spend my old age alone. Who will visit me in the nursing home? Who will look after my possessions when I die? Put flowers on my grave? Who will feed my cats, water my plants?

We stake our claim to immortality through our children. We aim a collection of our genes at eternity. Through them we hope to be kept alive in memory.

I will have no descendants to keep me alive, in memory or genetics. On my family tree I am a terminal bud. A biological *cul-de-sac*. A genetic dead end.

By choice.

Lesléa Newman

Of Balloons and Bubbles

I am not a mother by choice, meaning I have chosen not to be a mother, as opposed to Maria, who is also not a mother by choice, meaning she is a mother though she did not intentionally choose the position. Maria merely fell in love with Stephanie, who three years down the road announced that she was going to have a child. And so she did.

Now it is two and a half years since Frannie came into the world and Stephanie has had to take a part time Saturday job in a music store to help pay for Frannie's day care. Which means Maria has to watch Frannie on Saturdays. And it's not that Maria doesn't love Frannie to pieces, you understand. It's just that having a child was never in her scheme of things and every once in a while Maria longs for a luxurious Saturday afternoon where she could practice her viola in peace (she and Stephanie met in a music theory class), or hang out with a friend downtown over a cup of cappuccino, or even go grocery shopping without her two and a half year old angel taking every box of cereal off the bottom shelf to see what's inside.

And that's where I come in. You see, as my biological clock continues to tick away like that obnoxious stop watch on *Sixty Minutes*, I've been reconsidering my decision. Lately, every once in a while (I suspect when I'm PMS) I experience a strange longing to hold a baby in my arms, to rock a child to sleep, to bake cookies and pour tall glasses of milk. Lately I've been wondering what my daughter would look like (she's always a daughter in my fantasies). Lately, visions of me sitting peacefully in a rocking chair with a cup of tea, my little bundle of joy blissfully asleep beside me, have been dancing through my head.

Usually when I am in this particular mood, I pop over to Maria and Stephanie's house and Frannie obliges me by sitting on my lap and hearing my latest rendition of *Green Eggs and Ham*. Today, though, my hormones must really be going wild, for I have spent the entire morning at Caldor's, not buying the plastic and window caulking I need to get my apartment ready for winter, but oohing and aahing and even shedding a tear or two over the tiniest, sweetest pair of black patent-leather Mary Janes you've ever seen. Then I went home and called Maria with a daring proposal: I offered to take Frannie off her hands for an entire Saturday afternoon. It's time for me to really try out this motherhood business once and for all, I told her. And she agreed.

It is a gloriously sunny, crisp, New England afternoon, the kind we Vermonters remember on sub-zero January days when we're wondering why in the world we live in this state. I am going to take Frannie to a farmstand to pick out a pumpkin and then we're off to the park for a rollicking afternoon on the swings. Or at least that's the plan.

I arrive at one o'clock, as prearranged with Maria. "Hello," I call as I push open the door. "Anybody home?"

"Nomi! Nomi!" Frannie comes tearing into the front hallway wearing nothing but a yellow T-shirt that says GIRLS ARE GREAT on it. "Nomi!" she shrieks again, quite pleased with herself, as she has just learned to say my name two weeks ago.

"Hi, Frannie-pie. Ready to go?" A rhetorical question, as Frannie obviously can't go out in the October air, glorious as it may be, without her pants on. I squat down and give her a hug. "Where's Maria?"

"'ria! 'ria!" Frannie races through the living room which is scattered with building blocks, the colored rings of a stack toy, several picture books, a teddy bear and Frannie's bottle.

"Hi Naomi." Maria emerges from the bedroom waving a pint-sized pair of panties. "Frannie, you ready to put these on, or do you want to try the potty again?"

"Potty." Frannie runs into the bedroom and disappears, presumably to perch her tiny cellulite-free bottom on the potty.

"Excuse us," Maria goes in after her. "We're running on baby time here."

"That's okay." One of my shortcomings as a lesbian is always being on time, or worse yet, arriving early. I can see having a child would certainly cure me of that habit. "I'll just make myself at home," I call, flopping down on the couch, right on top of a graham cracker smeared with strawberry jelly.

I clean my jeans and sit down again, more carefully this time, just as Frannie gallops back into the living room, in her T-shirt and underwear. Progress is definitely being made. "Nomi, I pooped!" she announces, flopping down on the floor and picking up a block. "I build house."

"Frannie, here's your overalls, honey. Let's get dressed so you can go get a pumpkin with Naomi."

"Pumpkin! Pumpkin!" Frannie dances around the room with Maria following her, miniature overalls, socks, shoes, and sweater in hand. I am dazzled by this constant motion. Finally Frannie is ready and Maria's face sags with relief.

40

"Why don't you just take my car?" Maria asks, grabbing her keys from a hook on the wall. "The stroller's in the trunk and the car seat's all set up." She hands me the keys and a huge blue bag. "There's a set of clothes in there, a bottle of apple juice, some books, her stuffed piggy, whatever. I think there's some toys in the car, too. I'll walk out with you." She turns to Frannie. "Ready?"

"Up" Frannie raises her arms and Maria picks her up, for her 2.5 year old legs aren't quite long enough to navigate the steep back steps yet.

We get to the car and Maria buckles Frannie into her car seat, tucking a bottle, a plastic set of car keys, an elephant puppet, a small Kermit the frog, and a Sears catalog around her, even though the farm stand is a mere five minutes away.

"Isn't she a little young to be thinking about washing machines?" I ask as Frannie immediately goes for the Sears book.

"She loves the pictures," Maria replies, putting the blue bag in next to Frannie. "There's a hat in here in case it gets windy, but I don't think you'll need it. Bye-bye Frannie-love. Here's a kiss." Maria gives Frannie a hug and a kiss and starts to back out of the car.

"Kiss Goofy," Frannie says, kicking her foot up and extending the plastic Goofy bow-biter on the edge of her shoelaces.

"Bye, Goofy. I'll blow him a kiss." Maria kisses her own palm and blows in Goofy's direction. "Here's one for Son of Goofy." She blows a kiss towards Frannie's other foot, straightens up and closes the car door. "Bye, you two. Have fun." She stands on the edge of the driveway while I start the car and shift into reverse.

"My painting hurts," Frannie calls from the back.

"What, sweetie?"

"My painting hurts."

"Your painting hurts?" What could that possibly mean? I put the car back into park and swivel around in my seat. Maria, smelling trouble, walks back to the car.

"Her painting hurts," I inform Maria.

"Your painting hurts?" she asks, opening the car door again.

"My painting hurts," Frannie repeats loudly, frustrated, I imagine, by the non-intellectual life forms she is dealing with here.

"Your painting hurts," Maria says to Frannie. "Show me where."

"Here." She points under her bottom and squirms in her seat.

"Let's see." Maria lifts Frannie to reveal a crumpled up piece of scratchy art work. "Did I put you down on your painting? Silly me. I'm sorry." She removes the painting and buckles Frannie in again. "There, that's better. Everything hunky-dory now?"

"Yeah." Frannie settles in and puts her bottle in her mouth.

41

"Bye." Maria waves as I back out of the driveway without incident. It is 1:45, according to the clock on the dashboard. Not bad, I suppose, for baby time.

"Look at the leaves, Frannie, aren't they pretty?" I say, pointing out the window.

"Yeah," Frannie answers, dropping her bottle. Yeah is her favorite word. "My bottle. My bottle, Nomi." I look in the rearview mirror to see her reaching for it, straining against her seatbelt.

"Hold on, Frannie, I'll get it." I reach behind my seat, keeping one hand on the wheel, feeling for the bottle with the other. Thank God Maria has an automatic I think, as my fingers brush the bottle, sending it further out of reach. I contemplate pulling over, but with a little twist I manage to retrieve Frannie's bottle and undo fifty-five dollars worth of chiropractic work at the same time. Oh well. "Here you go, Ms. Frannie." I extend the bottle to her and make a wide right turn. Now we are on Route Fifty-Seven, a beautiful country road.

"We're almost at the pumpkin patch," I sing out, opening my window a little. "Umm. Doesn't the fresh air feel good, Frannie?"

"Yeah," she says, this time both hands holding fast to her bottle.

"Here we are." I pull the car over to the side of the road where a long line of cars has parked. "Look at all those pumpkins, Frannie." I point out the window. Orange spheres everywhere, large and small, as far as the eye can see.

"Pumpkins! Pumpkins!" Frannie pushes at her seatbelt with both hands. "I want out. Out!"

"Just a second, honey." I get out of the car and walk around to the side away from the road to free Frannie. She's off like a shot, yelling, "Hi pumpkins! Hi pumpkins!" and waving her little hand with me trotting after her. The place is swarming with kids and adults, all buying pumpkins, gourds and gallons of apple cider.

"I can't." Frannie is pulling at the stem of a pumpkin twice her size, next to a sign that says DO NOT PICK UP PUMPKINS BY THEIR STEMS. "Nomi help. Nomi up."

"That pumpkin's a little too big, Frannie. Let's go look at the ones over there." I point to a large area of kid-size pumpkins and Frannie runs over with me at her heels.

"This one. This one." Frannie points excitedly at a huge orange plastic garbage bag with a jack-o-lantern face printed on it, stuffed to the gills with leaves. "I want this pumpkin." She flings her arms around it and tries to pick it up.

"That's not real." An older, and obviously more worldly little girl in a T-shirt that says Class of 2001 speaks solemnly to Frannie. "That's not a real pumpkin," she repeats, this time to me.

"Well, thank you for pointing that out," I say, my voice just as serious. I squat down and pick up a fat little pumpkin. "How about this pumpkin?" I ask Frannie, holding it out to her.

"No."

"How about this one?" I offer another.

"No."

"Ooh, look at this one. See what a nice curvy stem it has?"

"No."

"All right, "I'm no fool. This could go on all day. I straighten up, my knees cracking. "I guess we won't get any pumpkins, then," I say, sounding more than a little like my own mother.

"Pumpkins!" Frannie trots across the farmer's yard to an old fashioned wagon filled with gourds. "Up," she says, lifting her arms to me.

I pick her up, praying that my chiropractor will have an opening this week, and point to the gourds. "See, Frannie, these are gourds. There's green ones, and yellow ones . . ." I pick one up to show her. "Sometimes there's seeds left inside and you can make a sound with them." I shake the gourd but nothing happens. No matter though, as Frannie is not in the least bit interested in my music lesson. "Pumpkin!" she yells, shattering my ear drum and squirming out of my arms. "My pumpkin. Mine." She reaches toward a small round orange gourd.

"That's not a pumpkin, honey. That's a gourd. It looks like a pumpkin though, doesn't it?" I grab it off the wagon and hold it up. "See, it's round like a pumpkin, and it's orange like a pumpkin . . ." I gesture toward the zillions of pumpkins surrounding us and Frannie snatches the gourd out of my hand.

"My pumpkin," she croons happily. "My pumpkin."

"But Frannie." I don't know what to say. Obviously the child is in love and who am I to spoil it for her. But then again, was I screwing her up for life by letting her believe something was what she wanted it to be, rather than what it really was?

"Okay. Let's go give the farmer a quarter." I put Frannie down and we walk over to a man in a plaid shirt and overalls, with a white cloth money bag tied around his waist. After all, she isn't hurting anyone with her little delusion, I reason with myself. And life is full of disappointments as it is.

We make our purchase, get back in the car and turn around to head for town, our destination being the schoolyard, also known as the park.

"Oh look, Frannie. A fair." I nod my head out the window toward the town common, where autumn festivities are in full swing. There's

43

craft booths set up and a band and a big food tent. A banner stretched across the road proclaims: AUTUMN FESTIVAL, SATURDAY OCTOBER TWELFTH. "Want to check this out, Frannie?" I ask.

"I want a balloon," Frannie says, reaching toward a bunch of orange, yellow, and red balloons tied to a tree bordering the commons. "My balloon, my balloon," she calls as we drive by.

"One balloon for Ms. Frannie coming right up." I take a left turn and look for a place to park. The street is jammed and I finally find a space three blocks away.

"We'll have to take the stroller, Frannie-pie," I say, shutting the ignition. "This is a big walk." And I know for a fact my back cannot possibly withstand lugging an extra thirty-something pounds up this hill.

I leave her in the car while I open the trunk, take the stroller out and try to figure out how to uncollapse it. It somehow works on the accordion principle, I know, like those old-fashioned wooden drying racks, but I can't seem to get the sides straightened out and even. I'm working up quite a sweat here, so I take off my jean jacket and fling it into the back seat next to Frannie. "You're being so nice and patient," I say, giving Frannie, with that one remark, more positive reinforcement than I received in my entire childhood. "Just one more second and Aunt Naomi will get it together." I wrestle with the stroller again to no avail. Finally I see a man and a woman with a Frannie-sized child in a similar contraption coming up the street. I swallow my butch pride and ask for help.

"Here." The man pushes a lever on the side of the wheel, snaps the stroller open and locks everything in place. "Just pull this to fold it up," he says, flicking the little lever.

"Thanks," I say. I was kind of hoping for the woman's assistance, as a good role model for Frannie, but oh well. Instead of fussing with the stroller, she walks over to the back of the car, pokes her head in and pokes it back out. "How old is she?"

"Two and a half."

"What's her name?"

"Frannie."

"Hi Frannie. Are you going to the fair?" She reaches into the car and strokes Frannie's hand. "Oh, what nice, soft skin you have. What a nice, soft hand." The woman straightens up and says to me, "God, remember when we had skin like that?"

We. Not only can I not remember my skin ever being butter-soft like Frannie's, but I also cannot remember the last time a straight woman lumped me together with herself into a collective pronoun. Maria says having a kid is like being let into this secret club; straight women talk to her all the time now. Until of course they hear Frannie call her "'ria" instead of Mommy, and ask her why and Maria explains that she is Frannie's co-mother, her lover Stephanie is Frannie's birth mother. Then they usually just nod politely, and clutching their own child, hastily slink away.

"Let's go, honey." Father and son are impatient, though I sense Mom would be happy to stand around chatting all day.

"Bye-bye, Frannie." The woman waves and Frannie waves back. "She looks just like you," she says, ambling away with her family. Strange, Maria says people say that to her all the time, too. I laugh and take it as a compliment as I duck into the car to remove Frannie. Before she can demand to walk, I buckle her into the stroller and we're off.

The fair is mostly local craftspeople selling patchwork quilts, stoneware pottery, wooden pull toys, crocheted booties and sweaters, and fresh honey, along a narrow midway of tents and booths. There's a bluegrass band playing over by the food tent and three black dogs of various sizes, all with bandannas around their necks, are frolicking in the grass. People mill about, looking at the crafts, eating hot dogs and generally enjoying what is undoubtedly one of our last truly warm days for at least six months. I crouch down to unbutton Frannie's cardigan, for in the sun it is almost hot.

"I want out. Out, Nomi," Frannie says. "My balloon."

"Okay, honey. Let's go find your balloon." I take her out and we walk along, pushing the empty stroller together. "There's the balloons," I say, pointing to the far end of the crafts aisle where a bouquet of balloons wave in the air. We make our way over to them, steering the stroller around people, dogs, tent poles and table legs.

"What color do you want, Frannie?" I ask, looking up at the bunch of balloons in the sky. "See, there's red, yellow, green, purple, blue . . ." I turn from the balloons toward Frannie, but she is no longer at my side. "Frannie? Frannie!" I turn around, my heart thumping wildly, my imagination already picturing her dear little face on the side of a red and white milk carton: "FRANNIE MATTERAZZO-HARRIS, LAST SEEN OCTOBER TWELFTH . . ."

"Frannie!" I yell again, relieved to spot her not ten feet away, her hands covering her ears. I desert the stroller and go to her. "What's the matter, honey?" I squat down, my knees cracking again. "Are you scared, sweetie-pie?"

"Yeah." She doesn't take her hands away from her ears.

"Are you afraid the balloon will make a big noise?" Maybe she'd accidentally popped a balloon once.

"No." Frannie shakes her head vigorously.

45

"What then, honey? Should we forget about the balloon?"

"My balloon." She reaches one hand out tentatively, then claps it back over her ear again as a woman with green frizzy hair and a big red nose comes over to us. She is wearing a pink and yellow checkered clown suit, with enormous purple sneakers on her feet.

"Hi there, little girl. Would you like a balloon from Emma the Clown?"

"No!" Frannie shrieks, puncturing my other ear drum. She collapses into a fit of sobs and I sit cross-legged on the grass, pulling her into my lap.

"Whoops. Sorry." The clown backs away toward her helium tank where a young customer is waiting.

"Are you scared of the clown, Frannie?" I ask, holding her tight.

"Yeah." She punctuates her answer with a howl I'm sure Maria hears back in their apartment. I rock Frannie on my lap, wiping her face gently with the end of my sleeve, since of course I don't have a tissue or a hanky on me. She continues to cry softly as I ponder the situation. I could say to her, it's all right, Frannie, clowns are fun, they're not scary, but that wouldn't help her trust her own instincts now, would it? So maybe it would be better to agree with her, and say, yes Frannie, that's a very scary clown. But would that make her even more fearful and ruin her chances of ever enjoying a trip to the circus or a parade? I sigh and stroke her fuzzy head. What's a mother to do? I decide to go the route of my own mother and sidestep the issue of Frannie's feelings in favor of offering a practical solution.

"You wait right here, Frannie, and I'll get your a balloon, okay? You sit here and I'll deal with the clown, all right?"

"Yeah."

"I'll be right over here by the balloons, see? I'm only three steps away, okay?"

"Okay."

I ease her off my lap and hobble over to the balloons, as my right foot has fallen asleep. "What color do you want, honey?" I call.

"I want red."

"Okay. Stay right there." I keep an eye on her while the clown fills a red balloon with helium and ties it to a long white string.

"Here you go." Frannie takes the balloon's string from me. "Come, let's go to the park." I start pushing the stroller and she scoots under my arm.

"Frannie push," she says, holding onto the stroller. Immediately her balloon takes flight, soaring skyward toward balloon heaven.

"My balloon. Bye-bye balloon." Frannie waves, fascinated for a moment. Then her lower lip starts to tremble and her eyes fill.

46

"I'll get you another one," I say quickly. "Let's go back to the balloons." Again I leave her and the stroller three steps from the clown who is handing a green balloon to a little boy's mother. She takes it, ties a slip knot in the string and loops it around the little boy's wrist. Oh, right, I think as I order another balloon. Of course you don't hand a helium balloon to a child. You attach it to them. Fortified with this new knowledge, I take the balloon to Frannie and tie it to her wrist. "All set?" I take a few steps with the stroller.

"Frannie push." She buts her head under my arm and takes over.

"Okay." We proceed until she crashes into the tent pole of a woman selling windchimes and stained glass window ornaments. The collision creates quite a musical racket, but nothing breaks, thank God.

"Frannie, it's too crowded for you to push the stroller by yourself." I put my hand on the stroller, which she promptly pushes away. "Do you want to ride in the stroller?"

"No. Nomi ride. Frannie push."

"I'm too big to ride in the stroller, honey," though at this point, believe me, I do appreciate the offer.

"Balloon ride."

"You want your balloon to ride in the stroller?"

"Yeah."

"Okay." I slip the string off her wrist, secure it around the stroller and set the balloon in the stroller seat. "There, how's that?" I let go, and the balloon, being full of helium, bobs up, straining at its string.

"Balloon ride," Frannie insists, reaching up for it.

"Sweetie, the balloon can't ride. It's full of helium," I say, wondering what in the world that can possibly mean to a two and a half year old child. "You want to hold the balloon again?"

"Yeah."

I untie the balloon from the stroller, and noticing Frannie's wrist is a little red, I tie the balloon to the strap of her overalls. A vision of Frannie floating up to the treetops like Winnie the Pooh crosses my mind, but she stays firmly rooted to the earth.

"How's that?" I ask.

Frannie looks up. "Hi balloon," she sings out, waving. We push the stroller together and she doesn't move my hand away until we have taken five whole steps.

"Frannie, I have to help you push the stroller. It's too crowded here for you to do it by yourself."

Frannie lets out a wail. "No. Frannie push. Nomi go away."

I am cut to the quick. Rejected by a two and a half year old? "What's wrong, Frannie-pie?" I wonder if she's still a little flipped out

47

over the clown. Maybe there's a load in her pants? Nope. Could she be hungry? "You want a hot dog, Frannie?" I ask, wiping her face with my sleeve again.

"Yeah," she sobs.

"Let's go then." Two more steps and Frannie again slaps my hand from the stroller.

"Frannie." My voice is firm, yet loving, I hope. "Here's your choice: you can either ride in the stroller or let me push it," I say, not giving her a choice at all, a handy trick I picked up from Maria. Frannie continues to scream and cry as I buckle her into the stroller, acting like the countless parents in supermarkets I have always glared at with disapproval in the past.

We make our way over to the food tent, Frannie's balloon hitting me in the face with every other step. She continues to howl and I ignore the stares, real and imagined, being thrown our way. I park her at the entrance to the food tent. "Hang on, honey, I'm right here. One hot dog coming up." As soon as I take two steps up to the table, Frannie quiets down.

"You want ketchup or mustard?" I say over my shoulder as a woman hands me a hot dog.

"Ketchup," Frannie says.

I squirt a thin red line down her bun, sidestep a swarm of bees, and stuff my back pocket with paper napkins before returning to her, pleased with myself for finally catching on. "Here." Frannie takes the hot dog and I retreat behind the stroller, ready to head out. Two steps later a howl reaches my ears.

"What now?" I lean down toward Frannie.

"Bumblebee." And there is her hot dog on the grass with two bees crawling around the bun.

"Let's just go to the park," I say. "I'll buy you something to eat on the way." I reach into my back pocket for a napkin, marveling at the fact that even though Frannie never took a bite out of her hot dog, she did manage to get a glob of ketchup in her ear. I wipe her face and steer her back to the car, stealing a glance at my watch. How can it possibly be only 2:35? I can't take her back to Maria's yet. We haven't even been gone an hour.

I open the car door and a gust of heat hits me in the face like hot air from a blow dryer. I buckle Frannie into her car seat, untie her balloon, retie it to the handle of the back door, open the window of the driver's seat, collapse the stroller, stash it in the trunk, pop Frannie's bottle into her mouth, slide behind the wheel, start the car, and head for the park.

"Window up," Frannie says from her perch in the back.

"You want the window up, Frannie?" I roll it up, then crack it, as the air in the car is really stifling.

"Window up. Window up." Frannie's high pitched voice is reaching new heights.

"Honey, I have to have the window cracked. It's ninety-eight degrees in here."

"Up. Up!" Frannie is screaming.

"Are you afraid your balloon will fly away again? I tied it." Frannie is screaming too loudly to hear me, but nevertheless, I continue. "Are you afraid a bumblebee will get into the car?" Frannie yells even louder. I roll the window down a little more to let the sound out. "I'm sorry, sweetie, you can't always have things your way." Now I sound exactly like my mother. Oh well. She always did say when I had a child I would understand.

I drive by the schoolyard a.k.a. the park, only to find half the grass dug up and a noisy yellow tractor moving along on its gigantic wheels. I am a little disappointed and a lot relieved. "Looks like the park's closed today, Frannie. We'll have to go home."

"Swings. I want swings." Frannie points out the window.

"Sorry, toots. Not today. We'll have to go on the swings another time."

"Swings. Swings." She continues to cry as I steer the car back to Maria and Stephanie's, one hand on the wheel, one hand stroking her leg. Finally, one block from home, when I think my head is just about to implode, Frannie falls asleep.

I pull into the driveway and open the car door as quietly as possible. Frannie is dead weight in my arms as I lift her out of her car seat. I nudge the door with my hip just at the moment that Frannie's balloon decides to peek its stupid little red head out of the car. Of course the door shuts right on it.

I hold my breath as the noise startles Frannie's eyes open. All is quiet for one lovely second and then all hell breaks loose.

"Go ahead and cry, Frannie," I say, hoisting her onto my hip. My own eyes fill as well, for it is not only Frannie's balloon that has burst, but my own bubble as well. Being a mother isn't all it's cracked up to be, I realize, but much, much, much, much more, and I'd only tried it for an hour. I ring the bell to Maria and Stephanie's apartment. No answer. Stephanie is still at work, I know, and Maria is probably out enjoying the precious freedom I take for granted.

I walk with Frannie over to a little patch of grass beside the driveway and sit down to wait for someone to come home. I am absolutely exhausted. I guess my choice not to have a child is the right one after all, I think, looking down at Frannie who has just fallen back asleep with her head on my shoulder and her arms around my neck. I stroke her back and she sighs contentedly, clinging to me as my heart turns over, heavy with the dearness of her and the weight of my choice.

Carolyn C. Emmett

Learning How

Yellow leaves in sudden flight
rain drops lightly
Still learning how
I accept
this yellow-leafed Fall

I find myself watching
a father and daughter embrace
such a gentle kiss upon her face

so purposefully childless
I recognize
a love I never had
nor can recall

Against my window pane
now
a sudden heavy rain

Terri de la Peña

Nullipara, 44

While I sit in the university's obstetrics/gynecology waiting room, the talk around me is of babies, recently born or about to be. I page through *Off Our Backs*, scanning articles about reproductive rights, silently bleeding.

"When is yours due?"

"End of April."

The pregnant women, one blonde, the other Latina, smile to each other, sharing a commonality they perhaps would not find beyond this mauve and pink room. The Latina tentatively glances in my direction, her dark brows lifting.

I anticipate her question. "I've been bleeding for six weeks."

"I'm sorry," she says.

"Hey, I'm 44. It happens."

"Do you have—any babies?" she whispers. The blonde has gone back to her *Parents* magazine.

"No. Never wanted any."

The Latina stares as if I have uttered a blasphemy. And, coming from the same Catholic-steeped culture she undoubtedly was raised in, I suppose I have.

"Mrs. Yniquiz, the doctor can see you now." A nurse gestures towards her. Mrs. Yniquez averts her eyes and rises to follow the nurse. I pick up my news journal, and its words blur before me.

I am two and a half years old and Mama is in the hospital. While she's gone, I am scared of the dark. My big sister swears the bogeyman hides in our bedroom closet. To keep him away, I ask to sleep with Grandma. She scolds my sister and lets me crawl into her narrow bed, all the while worrying about squashing me.

"But I'm little, Grandma." I snuggle next to the wall. "See? I won't even move."

Grandma tucks me in and lies beside me. "Esta bien." She whispers so she won't wake the others. "Maria Teresa, ahorita tienes una hermanita, and your mama will bring her home soon."

"But I don't want a little sister."

She smiles and smoothes the dark hair from my brow. "It's not up to you mijita. You'll learn to love the baby."

I shake my head vehemently.

"Mira, que caprichuda! Now don't be a bad girl."

"I'm *not*."

She considers this briefly, before kissing me. "Go to sleep, eh? Es tarde."

That night, the bogeyman stays in the closet and I cuddle next to Grandma. Her flannel nightie is soft and smells good. I am safe with her and won't dream about Mama. She's so mean to bring home a bratty baby. I'm the baby in this family, no one else.

But Grandma is right. After being away from Mama, I start missing her and wind up letting her hug me when she comes home. When she shows me the baby up close, I see my hermanita's skin is light, not brown like mine, and her hair is not as dark either. She makes funny sucking noises and moves her itty-bitty fingers in jerky ways. And I guess she's really not so bratty after all, even if her face gets red and scrunchy when she cries. Before long, we become best friends.

I am seven years old and, again, Mama is coming home from the hospital. She is bringing my newest little sister. Daddy is too busy to talk to us, so Grandma tells my hermanita and me to behave ourselves, not to make a lot of noise, because baby Patty needs to sleep a lot. She was born on St. Patrick's day, and I imagine Patty with a green velvet bow in her hair, a baby-sized shamrock clutched in her tiny fist. I even wonder if she wears green diapers.

But Patty doesn't look Irish at all. She has black hair that stands on end, a round pink face, and funny, slanted eyes; she looks more like a Chinese baby than anything else. We peer over the makeshift crib, a wicker laundry basket, while Mama speaks in a quiet voice.

"Patty's a Mongoloid baby. That means she has a little brain. She's special, different from other babies. You both have to be very patient with her and help me take care of her."

I stare and stare at the sleeping infant. My hermanita is only four years old and doesn't pay attention. She wanders away to play with her dolls, but I stay near the baby.

"Why's she special, Mama?"

"Dios Nuestro Señor sends special babies to people He knows will love them. Patty's a gift from Heaven."

"But why does Daddy look sad?"

"He knows Patty needs lots of care. She won't be a smart little girl. She'll be very, very different." Mama's eyes are shiny and she takes my hand. "Ven conmigo. Let her sleep now."

"I want to stay here, Mama. I'll be quiet."

She nods and leaves us alone. I watch the dozing baby and wonder about Mama's words. Special, different—what does that mean? Patty looks Chinese, that's all. What's so special about that?

Wrapped in a paper gown, I shiver in the examining room. Gingerly I sit on the edge of the table, wary of staining its protective covering. Despite my offhand comment to Mrs. Yniquez, I worry about my month and a half of bleeding. Until reaching forty, I have never had menstrual problems, rarely cramps; for the past year, my cycles have been shorter and I have experienced right-sided headaches—creation pangs, I call them. Now this constant bloodshed—not only inconvenient, but also debilitating. I try to stay calm, to let my thoughts drift elsewhere.

Ubiquitous conversations about babies never fail to remind me of Patty. She is thirty-seven now, working with other developmentally disabled people in a workshop setting, living with our widowed mother; I am forty-four, a Chicana lesbian feminist writer, childless by choice. Growing up with a Down's syndrome sibling convinced me at a very early age that I did not want children of my own. People seem surprised that I so readily admit this. No one likes to hear that throughout my childhood my parents' attention remained on my "special" little sister, rather than on my younger sister and myself; my hermanita and I consequently escaped into a variety of fantasy worlds to cope with that sudden parental detachment. People would rather hear uplifting stories about our family's pulling together to care for Patty; for certain, we all did, but not without sacrificing some of our own needs.

When she became pregnant with Patty in the summer of 1953, my mother was forty-four years old, a devoutly Catholic wife and mother; my father was fifty. Statistically, their chances of conceiving a Down's syndrome child were high, but neither of them knew that. Chicano Catholics, particularly those of their generation, welcomed big families. Being from the working class, my parents were unschooled in medical facts; besides, medical researchers at that time knew little about what was then referred to as Mongolism. Even if prenatal counseling and amniocentesis had been available, my parents would not have taken advantage of such services. Their religious and cultural beliefs convinced them that bringing Patty into this world represented God's Will. In retrospect, I think otherwise, but I must admit she is the only child who will never leave them.

"When you've dressed, come into my office and we'll talk about the procedure." My doctor pats my arm gently as she leaves the examining room.

For a moment, I sit in stunned silence. Because I am bleeding so much she wants to schedule a D&C, dilation and curettage, to rule out cancer. At hearing that word, I tell myself not to panic. I do not cry; instead I am conscious of watching myself, looking for signs of emotional weakness. Robot-like, I reach for my clothes; I am cold and numb. Buttoning my shirt, I remember my older sister has had a similar history; that memory soothes me somewhat. I continue dressing, and before shutting the door, I glance behind me. The examining table's protective covering shows a large bloodstain where I had been sitting.

The doctor awaits me, the medical chart on her desk. I know what no doubt is at the top; "Para 0" or "nullipara"—medicalese for a woman who has never borne a child. That description makes me an oddity in this consultation suite. My first time here, I made my doctor laugh when she asked my birth control method; when I said "none," she asked if that was for religious reasons. I smiled and said, "No. I'm a lesbian." And she laughingly remarked that I was "lucky not to have to worry about all that." Since then, I have always trusted her.

Now I sit across from her, hands in my lap, the typical parochial schoolgirl pose I fall into by habit. I wish I could think of something funny, but my mind comes up blank. Instead, I listen to her explain a D&C is a routine outpatient procedure.

"Do you think I have cancer?"

"I want to rule that out. You're bleeding so much it's difficult to examine you today."

I nod and ask more questions. She tells me a D&C usually regulates one's periods. If it does not, she would consider short-term hormone therapy. In the meantime, she prescribes iron tablets to build up my strength. A few minutes later, I sign the consent forms and walk out. I do not see Mrs. Yniquez.

I climb the steps to my eighty-one-year-old mother's apartment. My tears finally come when I tell her about the scheduled procedure. She listens, even holds me briefly, but remains her usual detached self; she does not like emotional scenes. I feel her need for distraction: I am the family lesbian, the daughter she accepts but does not understand, the daughter who writes what should remain unsaid; I have learned not to expect more from her. Since my father's death, she seems even more unwilling to absorb anyone's woes. Religious as she is, I know she simply trusts in God and expects everyone else to do likewise. It is no exaggeration to speculate that she put herself on emotional "hold" the day Patty was born; I have sensed this since adolescence. Rarely have I seen my mother cry; I have always been the family "crybaby."

When she answers the phone, I get up. Her custom is to consider all phone calls priorities, no matter who is visiting. Whenever I complain about this, she tells me I am "too sensitive." Nerves on edge, I want to be alone to absorb the afternoon's events; I lack the patience to compete with her caller. I know that is a losing battle, so I leave. She waves as I walk out the door.

At home, I dial my older sister's number. When we were kids, she used to bully me, but at mid-life, our seven-year age difference matters little; she is the sister I am closest to now, the one I always rely on. She calms my fears and agrees to accompany me to the hospital on the scheduled date.

"You're just too young for this," she says.

"Weren't you my age when you had yours?"

She laughs. "Yeah. Well, it wasn't so bad. You"ll sleep right through it."

"Good." I hesitate a moment. "At this stage of the game, I know I'm supposed to mourn the fact that I've—"

"—never had kids?" she concludes. "Are you feeling that?"

"No. It baffles me sometimes, but I have no regrets. Do you?"

"Gosh, no. I used to hate babysitting you brats."

"It showed." I play with the phone cord. "I think some women just don't have the so-called maternal urge. It's weird that neither of us wanted kids."

Her voice is quiet. "Patty had a lot to do with that."

"Sure."

"My feeling is, sooner or later, Patty's going to be our responsibility. So it's just as well we didn't take on any more."

"Exactly."

After Patty entered our lives, my mother became more actively involved in parish activities. She was PTA President, Altar Society President, Guadalupana President, organizer of the school's hot-lunch program, fund-raiser extraordinaire; she seemed intent on being away from home as much as possible. Grandma was there to care for the baby and my teenaged brother and sister had their own lives; their memories of those turbulent times differ vastly from mine.

For my hermanita and me, those bewildering years drew us closer together. Perhaps to keep us from being underfoot, Daddy built us a backyard playhouse and we spent fun-filled hours there, playing with our doll families, creating complicated storylines, losing ourselves in that imaginary world, shielding ourselves from the pain of being overlooked and, eventually, from the grief of our grandmother's death. When she died, I was eleven years old, and since my mother was determined to continue her parish activities and my older sister had a full-time job, I inherited many of Grandma's responsibilities towards Patty.

A lesbian child, without a name for the difference I already sensed within myself, I resented having to care for my youngest sister. Preferring to play with our new puppy or curl up with an adventure story, I grew impatient with Patty's slowness, her short attention span, her limited communication skills, her inability to create imaginative games with us. Being with Patty seemed to stress my own feelings of difference; I knew no one else who had a little sister like her. I rarely spoke about her to my schoolmates; I wanted to erase her from my life.

But I could not escape Patty; she was an unavoidable part of our family. Whenever I voiced displeasure at having to take her to the bathroom or otherwise watch out for her, my parents labeled my behavior selfish and uncharitable. Their admonishments increased my burgeoning guilt about resenting Patty; in confession, I constantly mentioned "being mad about having to take care of my little sister." The priests counseled me to be loving and giving, to rejoice in being able to help the family care for Patty. They stressed that unless I accepted God's Will, as my parents already had, I would not pass muster on the Road to Heaven.

Oh, but what I would have given to hear my parents occasionally complain about the restrictions Patty placed on their lives! What seemed like optimistic attitudes to those outside the family, however, masked my parents' deep-seated denial. If Patty truly had been a blessing sent from God, why did my mother devote so much time to religious activities outside the home instead of concentrating on teaching Patty the basic necessities of life? Why didn't she cherish being with her "special" daughter instead of being obsessive about parish matters? And why did my father immerse himself in the daily newspaper and nightly television programs instead of spending one-on-one time with his youngest daughter? While I did not confront them with these questions—I would have been labeled impertinent and disrespectful—I sensed the pain beneath their outward demeanor. I only wished they would have talked about it with the rest of us, to let us know that they, too, sometimes resented Patty. If they had done so, I would have known that I wasn't being a "bad girl" by grumbling about baby-sitting chores; I would have known that I was simply being human.

Instinctively, though, I resorted to what I knew best—my imagination—to sort through the family's emotional quagmire. With my hermanita, I created a complicated scenario involving the extended doll family residing in our backyard playhouse: Lucy and Tom, the doll parents, had several children and ran a boarding house to make ends meet. A partially disabled construction worker, Tom had been injured at a job site and could no longer handle full-time employment. Among their boarders (besides the lady wrestlers and prospective actresses) were two young men: Tomas, a badly scarred burn victim (he was a rather bedraggled doll with a chipped face), and Danny, a cancer patient (a rubber doll I had mistakenly left in the bathtub too long). Both of these dolls not only had to deal with their physical disabilities, but also with outright discrimination from other boarders. Sometimes Lucy and Tom came to the rescue; other times, they were indifferent. Their actions seemed to mirror my ambivalent attitude towards Patty.

Thus, I shudder to admit we eventually buried both disabled dolls near Grandma's prized poinsettia bush. To recognize the wish fulfillment implicit in their elaborate funeral rituals chills me still.

The morning of the scheduled D&C, I do not think about those long-buried dolls. I only wonder what, if anything, lingers in the uterus I've purposely kept child-free. I feel very conscious of my age: the same as my mother's when Patty was born. My own life at forty-four, however, contrasts greatly with my mother's during the 1950s. I have made personal choices she finds incomprehensible: I call myself Chicana, lesbian, feminist, writer. At forty-four, she had her fifth child; I have just finished my first novel. I create with my brain, not with my womb. Other than our ethnicity and sex, we share little common ground. I know this frightens her; it saddens me. But, other than with words, I know no way to bridge the emotional chasm between us; she rarely reads what I write.

Awaiting my sister, I sit by the door, feeling strangely calm. My mother will not accompany us to UCLA Medical Center; she is needed at the parish this morning. Her announcement did not surprise me; like the rest of the family, I am used to playing second fiddle to the church.

My older sister arrives and drives me to the Med Center. "Are you sure you don't want me to wait?"

"It'll take up your whole morning."

"So I'll come back at 1:30—or later?"

"The nurses will phone you." I touch her hand. "Hey, I'll be fine. I just want this to be over."

"We found no cancer, " my doctor says. Without my glasses, I view her as a hazy, but smiling, figure; I grin sleepily and promptly forget whatever else she adds.

Afterwards I enjoy the attentions of the soft-voiced nurses; they hover over me, tuck me into warm blankets, speak soothingly. I seem to revert to childhood within this woman-centered environment; all I need is a couple of cuddly stuffed animals to complete the picture.

My mind wanders; I feel no pain, only relief. And, of course, I think about my mother, curious if she speculates about me as much as I do about her. She seems to remain unaware that my long-ago playhouse scenarios evolved into adolescent short stories, eventually becoming my current fiction writing. Does she realize that, unlike her, I do not feel obligated to have flesh-and-blood children? I am far more satisfied with my brain children. Through my lifelong experiences with Patty, I recognize that I lack the perseverance and patience to raise any child, differently abled or not. What my mother labels selfishness, I call self-awareness; what she labels selfishness, I call self-deception.

Yet, by her example, I have discovered life exists beyond motherhood; her constant need to be away from home, as frustrating as it is, has taught me that. She is feisty, strong-willed, humorous—qualities I share. And in many ways—though she would never admit this—she places her own needs first; I often do the same. Definitely, I am my mother's daughter.

When my sister appears at the doorway, I salute her with a brimming cup of coffee.

"A clean bill of health. Periods will be back to normal soon."

She strolls over to give me a hug. "I'm so glad. Ready to come home now?"

"You bet." I rise slowly, but steadily. "I have to get these kids out of my head."

"What?"

I laugh at her bewildered expression. "I have more stories to write."

Paula Amann

BREEDER

"Be fruitful and multiply!"
intoned the Voice
in the sparkling Place
of apples and serpents.

"Do you have a family?"
strangers ask as if
a baby were the only fruit
a woman of my age
and presumed fertility
would dare to give the world.

Families chromosomal and chosen
dance me through the seasons
as my birthdays lurch toward forty,
but I do not wake at four to nurse
a small, insistent mouth.

When I used to write songs
I dreamed of pregnancy,
the swollen belly of inspiration
that made notes and words
kick their way out of my heart,
yelling a life of their own.

Now I scribble poems;
I will overpopulate the world
with chiming consonants,
leave images red and wailing
on the doorsteps of the unsuspecting,
breed metaphors that fill the night
with flesh of chutzpah
and bone of hope.

Joyce Goldenstern

Childlessness

Like many stories, this story keeps changing. Like many decisions, the deciding comes first, the reasons come later.

Childlessness. It's a strange word. "Ness"—a state of being. "Less"—without. But our language, at least, has no other, less negative word—a state of being with?—that describes quite the same thing.

In 1979, when my friend Janet told me she had decided to get a tubal ligation, I wondered. I hadn't realized before that you could decide to get a tubal ligation. I guess that I had assumed—if indeed, I had ever thought about it before—that someone else made that decision for you. For medical reasons. For control. For punishment. I had heard about women in prison and in mental institutions. I had recently worked on a political event for Puerto Rican independence. I had learned about unsuspecting women in Puerto Rico who had been subjected to forced sterilization.

When Janet told me about what she was going to do, we were both 31. Janet was married. She had had two abortions. One legal, after Roe versus Wade, and one before, not. She and her husband wanted to adopt a child, rather than have one of their own.

Okay. Probably whoever was in charge of tubal ligations would think it made sense for her. Besides she had her husband to back her up. Had her husband to grant permission, in case that man in charge (I imagined a man) demanded another man's permission.

I didn't. I wasn't. I hadn't. And I might just as well have been 21 rather than 31. I mean, my life stretched before me like that. As though I would live forever. I had already had many jobs and adventures. I had hitch-hiked through Canada, for example. And taken a train to Mexico City. And taught English in Spain. I loved writing and riding my bicycle to my part-time teaching job. I loved savoring Chicago where I had recently moved. I loved taking my time, observing. I loved learning and political activity and working at idealistic jobs, just enough to support myself—no more. Maybe it would not be true to say I wanted my life to continue exactly as it was. But if I wanted it to change at all, I wanted it to change slowly, as it would—with no socially predetermined plan.

I have never felt driven to marry and have children. Even at 31, marriage seemed, at best, like something a long way down the road. Thoughts of having a family seldom entered my daydreams. Not even as a teenager. In my daydreams, I was usually living alone in a stark but pleasant room, surrounded by art, books, a radio playing classical music. In my daydreams, I was sitting at a huge wooden desk, writing. In my daydreams, my mate was an unobtrusive lover who would visit late in the evenings.

I tell you that I have never felt driven to marry and have children. But, of course, that's not the whole truth. I often have heard that shrill and persistent and censuring voice, "What the hell are you doing with your life?"

"I'm thinking of getting a tubal ligation," I told my boyfriend Jake. He was driving his orange '70 Volkswagen bug and I was sitting next to him, close enough to chart the response on his profile. His face changed. The thought was visibly upsetting to him. I'm quite sure not because he was thinking of any stake he might have in the decision. He didn't want to marry. He didn't want children.

"That seems drastic," he said. Or maybe he said "unnatural" or "unwomanly." I don't think he said "unwomanly," but somehow that thought came through.

"I'm tired of taking the pill. I feel like I'm poisoning my own body with it. Besides I just want to decide about something, to decide once and for all." Those were the reasons I would have given then. I can't remember if I actually gave them at that time. More likely, I quickly changed the subject. Or he did. I never told him—even though we stayed together for a number of years afterwards and then broke up and then got together again. I never told him. I never told my best friend at work. I never told lots of people. I had to tell one person though, because the out clinic required that someone pick me up afterwards. I told my friend Alice, because years before I had helped her when she needed an abortion.

But I'm getting ahead of myself. I couldn't get the tubal ligation immediately after the seed had been planted to do so. I didn't have health insurance and I didn't have the money to pay for the operation. Within a few months, however, I took a full-time job with the state of Illinois. I deliberately chose an HMO that included free tubal ligations as part of its benefits.

It all seems pretty willful, doesn't it? Thought I've never regretted the decision, I did go through a long period some years afterwards of wondering about myself. What was driving me? What had made me so determined? I still am not sure of the answers to those questions.

But determined I surely was. Even the HMO doctor did not deter me—though he very well might have. His face, like Jake's, changed when I brought up the idea. Historically, a stigma of abuse associated with female sterilization stains the medical profession. Coercive practices tied to eugenics and race purification abounded in the first half of the century and are still extant in some parts of the world. Not that long ago, doctors performed the "Mississippi Appendectomy" on black women in the South by tying their fallopian tubes without their knowledge. As eager as doctors have been to sterilize some women, they have been just as reluctant to sterilize others. Until 1970, doctors usually refused requests for voluntary sterilization from unmarried women or from women whom they did not feel had enough children. Sterilization committees at hospitals even devised an age-parity formula. The woman's age times the number of her children had to equal 120 in order for a sterilization request to be honored.

My HMO doctor bombarded me with questions, many of which were not medical in nature. I answered patiently. No, I had never been pregnant. Yes, I was sure I didn't want to have a baby. No, I didn't have a husband. And so forth. He stood above me, a tall, robust man whose very physical presence could have been intimidating. Strangely, though, I stayed calm.

After the interrogation came the horror stories. Something about how I might begin bleeding profusely years after I had the tubal ligation. I'm not kidding, he said that. I knew, then, he was simply lying for whatever reason of his own. I had done enough reading to know there was little risk involved in the procedure. Though his reaction angered me, anger was not the overriding emotion. I felt detached and if his irrationality had not been inconveniencing me so much, I might even have been amused that I had the power to threaten him so. The meeting ended with him saying the only way he would perform the operation is if I would see a psychologist first.

I wouldn't have minded going to a psychologist, but 1) seeing a psychologist through the HMO required a long wait, and 2) I didn't want a doctor so opposed to what I was doing operating on me. After thinking about it for a few days, I wrote a letter to the HMO to complain. Within four days, I received a phone call and an interview with the head of the HMO. She couldn't have been more apologetic or sympathetic. She did not question my motives, but simply assumed I had made a decision which was right for me. Within a few weeks, she had an appointment at an out clinic with another, non-HMO doctor set up for me. I felt very grateful.

Doctors use a number of procedures to sterilize, but by far the simplest and most frequent is laparoscopy. With laparoscopy, hospitalization is not necessary and recovery time varies from three days to a week. The laparoscopy I had was done under general anesthesia, but some women or their doctors prefer local anesthesia. My doctor used the two incision method. He made one tiny incision (about 1 cm. in length) near my navel and another just above the pubic hairline. A long thin viewing device was inserted through one of the incisions, so the doctor could locate the fallopian tubes, and then instruments for electrocautery were introduced through the second insertion. The actual surgery only took about twenty minutes, but I was in the clinic for about six hours. I stayed home from work for three days plus the weekend and was in bed for most of that time.

Physical or psychological complications linked to voluntary tubal ligations are rare. Scars from the incision are tiny and faint, and after a number of years disappear. Women continue to menstruate each month. The egg released by the ovaries is simply absorbed by the body. Most women who have been voluntarily sterilized report that they feel more relaxed about sex, but other than that notice no change in their sex drive. In some cases, it is possible to reverse a tubal ligation by undergoing a reversal operation. However, success of such operations is doubtful, so a tubal ligation should be considered an irreversible procedure. More information about sterilization can be obtained from the Association for Voluntary Sterilization, 14 W. 40th Street, New York, New York, 10018, 212-524-2344.

"Freedom is not in fragments. A non-fragmented mind, a mind that is whole is in freedom," says the twentieth century spiritual teacher Krishnamurti. "Freedom of choice denies freedom; choice exists only where there is confusion. Clarity of perception, insight, is the freedom from the pain of choice."

I think about this quote often. I think about it in relation to childlessness. I think about it in relation to women's liberation. I think about it when I think of my own determination to have a tubal ligation. As I have already intimated to you, I do not fully understand that determination. But I do feel having a tubal ligation was one of a few times in my life that I was acting with clarity and freedom. When I agonize over a problem and then make up my mind, I do not feel that same clarity and freedom. When I try to crowd all possibilities into my life, I do not feel clarity and freedom.

And isn't that what we often pressure ourselves to do? I mean, crowd all possibilities into a life. What is motivating so many women, aged 35 to 45 (and younger women, as well), who become obsessed with the need to have a baby before it's too late? I do not mean to diminish the complexity of that need. Nor do I mean to diminish the complexity of the need to have career recognition; nor the complexity of the need to feel sexually desirable; nor the complexity of millions of other—often competing—needs. But in the midst of confusion and choice, surely there should be a place for "lessness"—the state of being without. For paradoxically, nothing is surely something. Just as space in a painting is something. And space in the universe. A long walk on a leisurely day is not the same qualitatively as an exercise session between a business meeting and picking up the kids from day care.

This story, I have said, like many stories keeps changing. The deciding comes first, the reasons come later. The reasons elude; the reasons, like the story, change. At age 43, I suddenly for the first time in my life become intensely interested in science. I read ferociously. I read about chimpanzees and chaos and information and quantum mechanics and relativity and the human brain. I read science in the same way I have read literature, biography, psychology, history, and theology for many many years before I realized that science had something important to say to me too. I read subjectively. I read to find out my place in the universe. I read to find out who I am and why I act the way I do.

When I read about chimpanzees and evolution, I learn that the intelligence of a species has a lot to do with life span, especially the years lived after reproductive activity. Jane Goodall tells us that some female chimpanzees may live past child-bearing years, but female humans are by far the most successful females of any species at living long lives past menopause. Freed from the constraints of child birth and child rearing, older females help develop the intelligence of the whole species by passing on accumulated knowledge and wisdom. That's how the theory goes. I speculate and wonder. In an overpopulated world, do the childless serve a similar evolutionary function?

When I read about the human brain, I learn that scientists who measure brain activity with electrodes have found that our brains begin preparing for a moment of action long before we consciously decide to do anything. Quite amazing when you think about it. No wonder the reasons for our decisions keep changing. The reasons have very little to do with anything, in spite of our protestations to the contrary. But, then, what does have something to do with anything? A good question, isn't it? The astronomer Timothy Ferris speculates, "Perhaps [it] is the fate of all intelligence, everywhere—to act in ways it thinks are volitional, while never knowing whether instead it actually is playing a role in some unglimpsed master plan."

Reading about science can only make us wonder about, not know, the mysteries of life—those mysteries that we ourselves unwittingly participate in. That's how I feel about childlessness—that it is something of a mystery, surely just as mysterious and miraculous as bringing a child into the world.

I could also tell you, I often don't think about it at all. It is just part of the fabric of my everyday life. Sometimes I even forget that I have had a tubal ligation. I feel as sexual and as fertile as I felt at 16 or 21 or 31. In many ways, it is just not that big of a deal. I can say that without lying, but without telling the whole truth too.

I have told you that I have never regretted having a tubal ligation. And that is true. But that is not to say my life ended up happily ever after. When I am feeling alone or insecure, I look for understanding especially among other women who consider themselves liberated from constraints of gender conditioning. I don't expect to find understanding everywhere, but I feel especially depressed when I don't find it where I assume I will.

Once when I went for a routine examination at a woman's clinic, I saw a practitioner's face change in the same way Jake's and my HMO doctor's face had changed. I had just told her in response to a question that I once had had a tubal ligation. She just couldn't understand if I had never had a child, how I could have freely chosen to do such a thing. I hadn't expected to find such incredulousness at a woman centered clinic.

Once a good friend surprised me a similar way. We were discussing her decision to have a child at the age of 41. Although she was unable to become pregnant, she was going to try in vitro fertilization. "You know," she said, "even though you have had a tubal ligation, you could have a child that way too." The underlying assumption was that I must by now regret my decision, that anyone my age without a child must really want to have one.

Life goes on. The stories change. The reasons change. We learn. We speculate. We live with who we are, like it or not. Sometimes we find understanding, often we don't.

But today is a beautiful day in May. So, really, who cares about any of it? In my neighborhood pink and white blossoms perfume the air. Tulips, jonquils, lilacs, and bridal wreath mark the boundaries between modest bungalows with vibrancy and good will. In the park across from my apartment, young men amuse themselves by bouncing balls and insulting one another's mothers.

I write in that stark room I always daydreamed about. I have the wooden desk and lots of books. The rent is cheap. The walk to the corner store is not long and rather pleasant: along the length of

Kosciuszko Park, past a playground where agile urban children hang from their knees and walk on their hands, past benches where lovers hold hands and unkempt men and women drink alcohol from glass bottles barely disguised in brown paper bags, past the tennis courts where partners shout in Polish and Spanish, past the basketball court where Blacks and Latinos and whites compete for the nets, and today past a glorious cherry tree whose limbs are bent with the weight of rowdy nine-year-olds.

On my way back, I meet five-year-old Shawn, who lives in my building, and his friend Brenda. Shawn's skinny arms are hugging two huge branches of cherry blossoms. Leftovers, evidently, from the vanished nine-year-olds. Brenda carries a modest bouquet. "Look how they have hurt the tree," I say to Shawn and point to the jagged end of a rudely torn branch.

"They are for my mother," Shawn says, his face shining with unmitigated joy.

"You could have given her a small bouquet like Brenda's," I protest. But Shawn isn't listening. The day is too beautiful for lectures, no matter how well intentioned or deserved.

"Do you have any gum," he asks, smelling the peppermint on my breath.

"He really likes gum," Brenda adds. I take a pack from my pocket and offer a stick to Brenda and then one to Shawn.

"Thank you," Brenda says. "Thank you," Shawn echoes, though he usually forgets that nicety. I am about to walk on my way when Brenda says, "Happy Mother's Day."

Yes, that's right. Today is Mother's Day. Though I sent a card and gift to my mother a few days ago, it has completely slipped my mind. For a moment, I feel disconcerted by Brenda's good wishes so I laugh and shrug my shoulders. "Thank you," I say. "Happy Mother's Day to you guys too." Now they are the ones caught off guard by the greeting. So all three of us laugh. Then I wave good-bye; they wave cherry blossoms, and I walk back to my apartment alone.

Michele Patenaude

Saving the Earth One Less Baby at a Time

(This piece was first broadcast as an editorial spot for "That's the Way I See It," a radio commentary on WNCS in Montpelier on April 23, 1990)

The disposable diaper has become the dirty symbol of this country's garbage problem. Some people want to ban them. The diaper makers try to convince us that they can be recycled. Parents with pangs of environmental guilt are switching to cloth. Diaper services can't keep up with demand.

You might think that disposable diapers were a real threat to the planet. But let's face it: the problem is not the diapers; it's the babies inside them. We've got to stop having so many. The real threat to the planet is overpopulation.

One less baby means a lot less diapers. But more importantly it means one less drain on the earth's resources—one less mouth to feed, one less automobile to pollute the air, one less house to build, one less person to make babies 20 years down the road.

And if you think population is mostly a Third World problem, think again. One expert claims that each American child gobbles up the same amount of the earth's resources as do 20 to 100 children living in the Third World.

Fifteen years ago in this country, Zero Population Growth was a mainstream notion. Today population control is almost a taboo subject. Perhaps it's because of the rise of religious fundamentalism with its fanatical opposition to birth control and abortion. Or maybe it's because we of the Baby Boom Generation have finally entered our golden age of procreation, and we'd rather not be confronted with anything that would make us feel guilty about it.

Whatever the reason, the subject of population was glaringly absent in the hype about Earth Day a few years ago.

In *Fifty Simple Things You Can Do to Save the Earth*, that best-selling book that has become the environmental equivalent of the 10 commandments, there is not even a single suggestion on how to combat overpopulation.

Yet, you can compost, recycle, carpool and put bricks in your toilet tank until the cows come home, and it won't compare to the environmental benefits of bringing one less child into the world.

I suggest the addition of Simple Thing Number 51. It would be: "Don't have children. If you must have children—have only one. If you already have more than one—please stop now."

It's time we realized that having children is only an option, not a necessity. It's time we stopped being automatons when it comes to parenthood. It's time that we, as a society, begin to promote childlessness just as much and as well as we promote parenthood.

Indeed childlessness has a lot to recommend it. For one thing, you never have to change the diapers.

Valerie Chase

What are we going to hand to the children of the 21st century?

This piece was adapted from an interview done by editor Irene Reti with Valerie Chase in Santa Cruz, California.

I'm the oldest of six children. Between myself and my youngest brother there's nine years. We are all fairly close in age, and for the first 22 years of my life there wasn't a time when I wasn't around children. This was a very realistic setting to understand what the joys and the pitfalls of having children were. When I was nine years old my mother went back to work because prices were starting to skyrocket and our family needed two paychecks. I was old enough to take care of my brothers and sisters.

I love my brothers and sisters very dearly. My life would be a lot less rich without them. But being six children in the Sixties was something that wasn't very common. Most people were having anywhere between two, three or four children. Even though large families had traditionally been a very American value, our family, for the time, seemed large. People were starting to talk about zero population growth, and the population explosion of the planet. Our family would go out in public and people would just stop and stare. It was a sight people just didn't see anymore. We always were on display. We were a big family and we were told we had to be on our best behavior out in public.

Our family didn't have a lot of money but I don't remember times that weren't fun. We all played musical instruments and we enjoyed simple activities like barbecuing and going to the beach. The emphasis wasn't on material possessions, but on the fact that as a big group we could always entertain ourselves. As the oldest, I was very aware of the amount of hard work that my parents put into making sure that all of us were clothed, fed and got off to school: all of the responsibilities that come with children. Millions of diapers, lots of spilled milk, sibling fights, getting to see who got to ride in the front seat of the car. As we got older there were things like dental and doctor bills and keeping children in bigger sizes of clothing. I don't think there was a time as a child when I didn't understand what it would be like to be a parent. There was no room for thinking that having children would be an easy job.

My parents really wanted children. It was their dream to have a family of eight and they stopped at six when they realized what size family they could support. The Sixties and Seventies were a time of a lot of drugs and rebellion among teenagers and my parents put their time and energy into us. They didn't put it into their careers. They didn't put it into cars. They didn't compete with their peers for material possessions or prestige in their community. In my parents' eyes it paid off. But as someone who had to give up after-school sports to go and babysit my younger brothers and sisters, I was aware of the role that I played in their everyday care.

As a child and a teenager I couldn't envision having children of my own. It was a foreign idea. It didn't cross my mind. It didn't occur to me that my job in life was to reproduce myself. The most important thing to me as a teenager was playing music and being a part of our family. My mother wanted all of us to have a chance to be educated before we started a family, because she didn't have that chance and she saw that if we did that we'd always have something that couldn't be taken from us. I didn't see the need to question that assumption.

I was still in school until I was about 25. As a lesbian I wasn't focused on the idea of having children. In my late twenties some of my friends began to participate in the lesbian baby boom. Some of the first women in the country to think about being lesbian parents lived in Santa Cruz (California). I remember when my ex-lover and I were in a hot tub and we were having this casual conversation and all of a sudden she slipped in that she was thinking about having children and would I want to be a co-parent because she thought that I would be able to do a good job. I just remember being stunned because this was probably the first concrete realization I had had, in my late twenties, that no, having children was not something I wanted to do.

At about the same time, I was friends with a very good violinist. She and her husband didn't want children either. And it was really clear to both of us, because we play a lot of music in the community here in Santa Cruz, that if either of us had a child at this point in our lives, either the child was going to have to come to rehearsals or we would be at home. It would be unlikely that we would be at home so the child would probably have to be at rehearsals. I thought, oh my God, I can't even think of having a child because for the first time in my life I was really making a lot of musical progress.

I think most women go through a period in their thirties where they have to decide whether that little biological clock is going off, measuring the amount of time that they have left. If they really want a child it's the time to make the move. I'm 35. I can honestly say that

I don't think that clock is going to go off. I don't think it was ever set. At some point down the line when my brothers and sisters have children, I can be happy for them and I can be a good aunt, but I don't have regrets about my decision not to have children.

At one point I was living next to friends of mine, a lesbian couple, and they had just had a daughter. It has meant a lot to watch her grow up. My mother said to me. "Oh, this is wonderful. Why don't you want to have children?" I said, "Well you know, mother, I grew up in a big family. I don't feel the need to have children." My mother's response was, "Well I would have thought that would have made you *want* to have children." I know that a lot of children from big families think, "Family life is great! I want to pass on this experience." I spent the first 22 years of my life in a big family. I didn't have to replicate the experience I'd already had for what was possibly the first third or fourth of my life.

It's essential for people to realize that a complete life isn't made by having children. Family doesn't have to be biologically determined. When you love people and care about them, there are people beyond your biological family who become your extended family. I've been blessed with a whole group of remarkable people who have become my extended family. Part of being human is an extension of life beyond yourself so it's important to have strong ties to other people.

I am part Cahuilla Indian. When my ancestors walked this earth before non-Indian people invaded California and the United States, they raised children with a love for the earth that many non-Indian people just don't appreciate. Cahuillas understood that the land you walk on, that you live on, has to be respected, not desecreated—in terms of clean water, clean air, enough food to survive on. This is a time when the United States and much of our earth as we know it doesn't have these principles any more. We live in a place that's terribly polluted, a big hole in our ozone, toxic wastes that they want to dump on reservations and any place that the government can get away with. It's not an earth that you leave as an inheritance to your children. If you have a child today, in 1992, this child is going to live a major part of its life in the 21st century. Your child's life is never going to be qualitatively as good as, say, the life my parents started me off with in 1957.

What are we going to hand the children of the 21st century? We are handing them a big dump site, the earth as a place that's been used as a trash can. They will inherit problems that are ten times bigger than those that were here when I was born. I'm not saying that when I was born things were perfect. But life in the 20th century has gotten a lot worse.

I don't know how many people stop to think about that when they have children. Is having children just an act of pleasure for their own behalf? I know some people take the time and are really concerned with the responsibility of raising children. But I seriously doubt whether they've thought about the kind of world their children are going to inherit. I think if more people thought about this maybe there'd start to be less children in the world.

Beyond the problems of what children are going to inherit is the fact that when you look at childraising and how hard it is, there's a whole group of people that aren't fit to be parents. I don't understand why you don't need a license to be a parent. So many people have such misconceptions of childrearing. It's a lot of hard work, time and money to raise children.

Parenting is the hardest job in the world. You can do your best to instill the values that you really care about and that you believe in, but if your child wants to grow up and be a skinhead that's their choice. Ultimately you get a child that becomes its own adult mind. You have to let go of a child and let them become who they are going to be. I'm not willing to put in 18-21 years and then have some child of mine become an airhead, a video addict, or someone that wouldn't be a productive member of their community. Yet when you look at what's in the world these days—ecological destruction, violence, and an emphasis on materialism—I don't see how we expect to raise a generation of children with great values when they are surrounded by this society.

Finally, I don't see the point in putting a non-Indian in the world. Cahuillas are such a small group. I didn't grow up on a reservation, I'm an urban Indian. And it's awfully hard to meet another Indian. Indians are under a great deal of pressure. Of course you don't want to mix your blood. It's just another dilution. In three generations my family is at the point where I am down to being a quarter, instead of my grandmother who is a full-blooded Cahuilla Indian. Personally, that's not something I want to contribute to.

The values that are important to me, that I want to share with other people, are old and quickly becoming lost. I want to transmit the joy and elegance of playing a string instrument, with no electronic or computerized components. The other part of my life that means a lot to me is the ability to garden, to grow food, to raise beautiful flowers for people, and to make sure that my gardening in some way

continues to enrich the earth. I think these are two of the most important things that I can bring into the 21st century.

Shéree Anne Slaughter

Mother's Tears

This is a very ugly and dangerous world
To give birth to any child, boy or girl
Our of fear of them being pressured into a gang
Or living their life in a fast drug lane
Out of the fear of them breaking all of the rules
And refusing to go to any school
Out of the fear of them being out on the street
Unaware of the dangers that they might meet
Out of the fear of them having babies while they're too young
Out of the fear of them being rebellious against their moms
Out of the fear of them trying to be all that they can be
For a government that says "Come join the army"
The mothers' tears have flooded the cemetery lot
And I realize, I do not want what I haven't got.

Jyl Lynn Felman

Meditation for My Sisters:
On Choosing Not to Have Children

Prelude

I stop right here at the tip of my tongue:
In the middle of my wanting   more   of you
I stop right here at the tip of my tongue.

Can I tell you? Every time I call, before I even have a chance to say hello, you say, it's not a good time to talk. Jessie's sick today. Jessie's crying today. Jessie's hungry. Jessie's sleeping. Today.

Every time I call. You say it's not a good time. To talk. But you write that I have abandoned you. And withdrawn from your embrace. Silence and collusion. Your silence my collusion. Woman to Mother to child. To son. Your son Jessie. Who is hungry today.

You blame me for your own abandonment. You blame me. For my choice. For choosing not to have a child. For choosing not to have Your child with you.

I stop right here at the tip of my tongue:
In the middle of my wanting more I stop right here at the tip of my tongue. I have to.

It is not safe here among the mothers and their children. They cannot hear my version any more.

Jessie is sick. Today. Jessie is tired. Today.

You who are my friend, my beloved sister lover friend, how could it be otherwise? Didn't you know? I knew. I knew there would not be room enough. For both of us. Jessie is tired. Today.

Why can't we just say these things and continue? Each on her own way. Without the accusation. You and I. Let us each go. You have the child you so longed for. Now let me be. Let me go my way. With or without you.

I did not choose the separation that lives so raw between us.

From your womb to mine. Womb to empty womb. I did not choose this splitting deep between us at the root of who we are.

I stop right here at the tip of my tongue. I swallow and suck in. My wanting yearning hunger for your wanting yearning hunger. That is no longer mine.

I swallow and suck in. Before my mouth opens wide. Can't you take me with you? Did you forget so soon? To be left behind is excruciating.

I stop right here at the tip of my tongue. I swallow and suck in my wanting yearning hunger for your wanting yearning hunger.

I.

I keep searching back, farther and farther but the memory is always the same. I simply never wanted children—to bear my own, adopt or foster another human being into this world. For as far back as I can imagine, the longing women speak of has never been mine. Oh I have longings, deep cravings that could devour me if I let them. Ask me about my longings, probe me for my hungers. I want to love my woman lover/life partner openly—every moment of every hour of every day. I want for us to be embraced and for us to be the embrace. I want never again to suffer writer's block: the deadly silence that soaks me in wet terror night after night, draining my dreams, leaving me exhausted when I rise. I have many longings: that women be encouraged to speak not only the facts of our lives, but the truths of our daily existence. I have many longings that would all but consume me if I let them. I long for a full life—a life that is my own—as you my sister long for a child of your own.

When my biological sister had a baby, our already precarious relationship with each other became more vulnerable. I understood, then, the deep separation that has always existed between women who have children and the silenced, invisible and stereotyped women who make the choice to be childless. So I am writing about my choice not to have a child in order to become visible to you, and to break out of my own isolation. I cannot stand the separation between us any longer that leaves you feeling neglected and me feeling unworthy because I made a different choice: a choice not to have a child.

II.

Who am I? I am a lesbian visionary writer, activist, cultural worker, performance artist and a Jew. I am in a long term, committed relationship. I am about to publish my first collection of short fiction, *Hot Chicken Wings*. Although I have published essays, stories, and reviews it has taken me twenty years to finish my first book. There have been numerous interruptions in my artistic process. The most painful interruption was my inability to support myself and the debilitating effects of censorship as a result of family rage and the fury directed at me by some lesbians who opposed what I was writing about. Central to my particular struggle not to have a child has been the search for my own voice, including the desire to be heard, seen, and to articulate those truths that have remained nameless and invisible in my life as a woman. This journey for voice and vision has been an essential part of my life for as long as I can remember being alive.

At thirteen, I stood proudly before the congregation at Beth Abraham, as a Bat Mitzvah. For twenty minutes I discussed my interpretation of the weekly Torah portion. It was my first experience as a performance artist. For not only had I written the text myself, but also, I chose to fully dramatize my presentation with a passionate intensity I had been saving for just such an occasion. The moment I began to speak, I locked my eyes with the eyes of the congregation. From the bima, I spoke directly to my family, aunts, uncles and cousins, friends, and complete strangers. At thirteen, I turned to address the Rabbi with all the profundity of my youth. Facing the Rabbi, I knew I had a calling the way young girls express with total certainty the fact that some day, they will have children. I understood then, that to have voice—to be able to articulate specific issues, name questions, challenge the dominant reality and to tell stories—was what I was about. And I was terrified at what I felt was ahead of me. There were no guarantees.

My life has been consumed with what it means to find my authentic voice and to express that voice over and over again in various forms and contents. Risking accusation, silence and personal attacks, I continue to push through my own terror. Why am I telling you all this, when I am supposed to be writing about the decision not to have a child? I am telling you all this, because THIS informs every single decision I have ever made and will continue to make. The fact that at an early age—before I was ten—I imagined myself to be an artist, is a fact that infuses the whole of who I am and how I interpret my life including my relationships. Imagining myself to be an artist meant that

I knew intuitively that my life would be different—if I was actually to fulfill my own destiny.

In choosing to be an artist I did not know all the practical ramifications of my decision, but I knew that I had set myself apart from the expectations that society—white Anglo Saxon—and my own beloved people, the Jews, had for me. Slowly, I began to understand, almost imperceptibly at first then quite explicitly, how my decision to be an artist would effect every other part of my life. By fifteen I knew that I had called everything into question: marriage, motherhood, my ability to financially support myself, security, stability, and a life of predictability. When I decided to be an artist, I had called into question, without knowing it, the full parameters of what a woman is allowed to be. I did not know that in choosing not to have a child I would push the boundaries of my own womanhood for the rest of my days. I did not know that as I aged, I would feel less womanly, unfemale, or a neutered subject. In choosing not to have a child, as I age I also feel my womanhood burning deep within me: the hunger of my lust for a life I call my own. But in the end, I am left to authenticate my own womanhood without giving birth or directly participating in the raising of children. I cannot look to my womb for reassurance that I am fully female.

III.

When my heterosexual married sister had a baby, I had writer's block, insomnia, depression, homophobia. And fear. Lots of fear. When my cousins—all of them—started to have children, I felt sad, excluded and marginalized from their worlds, worlds that as lesbians, my partner and myself had only recently gained entry to. And when my friends, lesbians who swore they never wanted children, gave birth, I felt hopelessly abandoned. These friendships—our sisterhoods—have not survived the birth of children; our once shared visions of being family for each other—our own longevity as friends—has ceased to be relevant since my friends have been able to replicate the nuclear family model either by alternative insemination or adoption. I want to assure you that we were friends, deeply committed to each other before the birth of all these children. Twenty years ago we came out together, were each other's first woman lovers, discovered the future was gay and that we were the revolution. We dreamed together about making a difference.

Today, none of us has adapted well to the change that the children have brought. None of us including me. No matter how hard I tried, taking less and less with the expectation that I unequivocally

79

welcomed my friend's children into my life did not work for me. My lack of complete adoration for their children did not work for my friends. I understand, we could not tolerate each other's ambivalence. But still it hurts. In our terror we required absolute loyalty without question. So the women in my life who had children have found other women with children. And me, what have I found? I have found haunting questions that I ask myself over and over again: What does it mean to have rejected Motherhood/Mothering so completely? Where does it leave me? Who understands what I am trying to say?

The heart of the matter is that I have made a commitment to myself, to my creative powers until the day I die. This commitment is based on a relationship with myself that is not distracted by the dependence of another, vulnerable, human being. It means that the "I" of me can have no rival for my attention. For a woman, a Jew, and a lesbian, saying this is close to speaking heresy. It means that even in my relationship with my beloved partner there is a place of profound separation and autonomy that is not possible when there is the raising of children to attend to. Making the female "I" central, primary and primal is interpreted as arrogant and selfish. Ultimately it is viewed—out of necessity—as an untrustworthy position by those women who are mothers. But those of us who do not become mothers rarely have the clarity or sufficient ego to resist these negative stereotypes.

Yes, it's true. I have chosen not to sacrifice myself, my vision of what is possible for the world and my role in this process; I have chosen not to compromise and do less in order to raise a child. I believe in my ability to make a difference. I believe that I am a powerful person worthy of making a difference in my life time. And I believe that raising a child would not expand my particular vision in the ways that I want to expand. I have been able to authenticate myself without giving birth to another human being.

When my sister became pregnant, I noticed an immediate difference in the way she viewed herself and the world she inhabits. She had a sense of awe and wonder about everything. Touching the life growing inside her allowed her to touch a new place inside her self. Everything came into focus. Suddenly, her life had become sanctified because my sister was now engaged in creating miracles. From my point of view, my sister was able to finally access that place of wonder that lives so latent in most of us because she was pregnant. And within the mythology of pregnancy and motherhood, white women and their lives become instantly holy. The emptiness in my sister's life has been filled. Lurking here is the question that I do not feel permission to articulate: why is it that so many women I love cannot touch that place of holiness that lives within them until they become pregnant? Why isn't living life to the fullest each day, continually striving for that place of balance without children, awe-inspiring?

This discussion is not only about my sister, and her own, individual lack of fulfillment. The question I am trying to pose here is why women look to the birth of a child to give their lives meaning rather than looking inside, at themselves first. "What is missing?" does not seem to be a real question as long as having a child is an option. I do wake up at night terrified that my life has no meaning. I do imagine that I am all alone despite my life partner and my friends. I despair that my writing is meaningless; that I have made a huge mistake. But in my terror I do not long for a child, although I know that my despair would have an immediate answer if I did. Someone would need me. ME. Someone else's life would depend on me and the quality of loving attention that I could offer. If I am not careful, at this point in my ruminations all my self loathing sets in. I cannot imagine my own life, having no distractions from my calling, no excuses if I fail. No reason not to reach for the big picture.

But if I had a child to raise, I would have a viable excuse for not writing, not producing, and not pursuing a career. In choosing not to have children I have no excuses. I want you to understand that this is what separates us. You have an acceptable, guaranteed excuse not to do anything you don't want to do because you are raising children. You never again, if you choose, have to be direct with anyone about anything. Even yourself. Or me. I want to know how we can find our way back to each other. Do you want to find that way again? And what would we have to do differently to love each other as fully as I see you loving your children?

IV.

As I write about my choice not to have children, I realize that I am writing about my blood sister and all my other sisters who have or want to have children. It seems impossible to just write about my choice not to have a child, when so much of my reality and the choice itself is influenced by the women in my life who have children and the effect of the children on "our relationships—mother and nonmother—." I have noticed stages in the birthing process and how these stages impact on the adult relationships themselves. The pregnancy itself fosters a denial on both our parts that there will be any change at all. We continue to meet for dinner and talk about almost all the critical issues we love to talk about. There is an additional subject that we both tolerate to different degrees: the baby to be born. In this stage, both tolerate to different degrees: the baby to be born. In this stage, though, we are still assuring each other of our commitment to the friendship and that we will be able to work around the baby.

I dread that, because I know it/we will never be the same again. In fact, I view the choice itself as a statement of priorities. I do not know how to view "the choice" differently. I do not want to have an infant dependent on me. As an artist, I have never felt that having a child was an option. Accessing my own voice continues to be a difficult task. I want to put my wonder in different places than my womb. A child would be a profound diversion from this struggle. To choose an inward focus feels childish and immature. Financially, the realities of living my life as a writer make child rearing impossible. I live on the financial edge, dependent on the generosity of my partner. There is no way that I could even consider having a child while pursuing my career as a writer. I am almost forty. I am just beginning to access my voice, to tap my creative power. To have a child now would be to sabotage myself. I do not believe it is possible for a woman to be a mother and an artist simultaneously. And I am not interested in delaying any longer what has already been an infinitely long journey home, by giving birth to anyone but myself. Although the desire to be a mother is assisted and affirmed in infinite ways over and over again by the media, religious, cultural and political institutions, my desire to be an artist is not viewed as an essential visionary task, equally necessary for the healing and preservation of the planet.

Finally, I do not feel that the choice not to have a child is a choice that is entirely of my own making. It came with the territory of living on the edge. I am filled, though, with an enormous ache that is born from my sorrow at the disintegration of the relationships in my life between the women who have children and the women who don't. I do not know where it is safe to turn. There are questions I want to ask the mothers. But I stop right here at the tip of my tongue. There are questions I want to ask the mothers. But I stop right here at the tip of my tongue. I swallow hard and suck in.

82

Stephanie Harris

Voice of Truth

I
When she was young her mother's voice was gospel,
crushing her like a load of Gideon Bibles
dropped from the window of a sleazy hotel—

one with dead plants, bored bellhop
and a sickly red sunset through unwashed shades.

If this were a novel by Tennessee Williams,
her mother would die in that hotel
but take her sweet time about it:

her daughter would nurse her,
wither away, and yearn toward every male
that passed through the lobby.

She'd bring her mother iced tea or lemonade,
the latest movie magazines or romance novels
which she herself would later read with a flashlight.

This would be because she was overweight, clumsy,
full of hate and desire. The books and magazines would say:
men like girls who are versatile, pleasing, want babies
and are never angry.

II
At the age she is now, her mother had a job. She wore crisp blouses
and soft sweaters. Men at the office were crazy for her. She had
friends and parties, though she never drank and she went to church
on Sundays. After a suitable period of independence, her mother met
Father and married him. She quit her job, then night school. She had
babies. Life was heaven.

III
She must be crazy to give up all that. Her mother doesn't understand.
She tries to help her mother understand. Tries to forgive. Stays up all
night writing, trying to find her own voice.

83

Stephanie Harris

"Every day you fill him with soul-stuff, like a pitcher."
—Sylvia Plath

Dinner is a sacrifice:
the slain food and careful table,
as he pours his sorrows into her—
they fill her so full she can scarcely move.

Still, she takes him to herself, every evening,
over soup and salad, tipping the carafe of comfort
and strength into his glass, while her own stays empty.

There is nothing new or unusual about this—
her mother or grandmother must have done it also.

I, wide-eyed observer, took note, and vowed,
when I was grown, to pour
but one glass only, and that my own.

Contributors' Notes

Janet E. Aalfs is a six-foot one-inch white middle-class poet/martial artist/fiction writer/crane-tiger-seal, among other things. She is head instructor of Valley Women's Martial Arts and chair of the National Women's Martial Arts Federation. Her writing has been published in lesbian/gay and feminist journals and anthologies.

Paula Amann writes poems on Chicago's elevated trains in between non-profit fundraising, and singing in a Jewish klezmer band. She owes much to her writing support group, friends, family, and the Feminist Writers Guild. Her work has appeared in *Wyrd Women— Word Women, New Poetry,* and *Rambunctious Review.*

Valerie Chase is a classical violist and violinist, and rose gardener. She is 35 and of Cahuilla Indian/Mexican-American/Polish background.

Terri de la Peña is a Chicana lesbian feminist, celebrating her 45th year on Mother Earth with the publication of her novel *Margins* (The Seal Press, 1982). Her current project is *Territories,* a collection of short fiction about Chicanas and Chicanos in southern California.

Carolyn C. Emmett acts as a spokesperson and program coordinator of The Rockland Poets doing writing workshops and poetry readings in Rockland County, N.Y. Her poems dealt with Civil Rights and anti war subjects in the 60s publications. Currently, her poetry is concerned with nature, peace on earth, and for herself as a woman and an individual.

Jyl Lynn Felman is an award winning short story writer whose work has appeared in *Tikkun, Sinister Wisdom, Lambda Book Report,* and *Bridges.* Her stories are anthologized in *The Tribe of Dina, Korone Volume Six, Word of Mouth, Tide Lines, In a Loving Voice* and *Speaking for Ourselves.* Aunt Lute Books will publish her first collection of short fiction, *Hot Chicken Wings.*

Joyce Goldenstern lives in Chicago. Her fiction appears in many literary journals including *Quarterly West, Primavera,* and *Thirteenth Moon.*

Stephanie Harris is active in the Chicago-based Feminist Writers Guild. Her poems have appeared in feminist anthologies and small press journals; she performs her poetry in bars, coffeehouses, bookstores and the public library. Stephanie is a two-time winner and judge of *Rambunctious Review*'s Annual Poetry Contest.

Eloise Klein Healy's latest collection of poems *Artemis in Echo Park* was published by Firebrand Books in 1991.

Randi Locke, 37, is a program coordinator for a national religious organization consulting social justice activists on issues related to Israel, race and ethnic relations, and church-state affairs. Published in a number of anglo-Jewish publications, she is currently working on a book about Jewish defense groups.

Carolyn Morell is an Assistant Professor in the Social Work Program at Niagara University in upstate New York. She is 50 years old, has been married for 28 years and is intentionally childless. She is in the process of completing a book on childless women's lives for publication by Routledge.

Lesléa Newman's 12 books include *A Letter to Harvey Milk, Secrets, Heather Has Two Mommies,* and *Sweet Dark Places.* "Of Balloons and Bubbles" is taken from a recently completed collection of stories entitled *Every Woman's Dream.* Lesléa's newest novel, *In Every Laugh A Tear* is forthcoming from New Victoria Publishers.

Michele Patenaude lives in Vermont, is 38 years old, and enjoys not being a mother. She is a freelance writer and a college writing instructor.

Elissa Raffa, an Italian American radical lesbian, was born in the Bronx in 1959 but has lived since 1976 in Minneapolis. She writes prose and plays, teaches at Loring Nicollet Alternative School, and works with the Womyn's Braille Press and District 202: A Place for Young Queers.

Irene Reti is a 31 year old red-headed lesbian, the publisher of HerBooks, and the daughter of two Jewish Holocaust refugees. She has known she didn't want to have children all of her life and does not think of her cats or rose bushes as child-substitutes.

Nina Silver is a therapist, Reichian bodyworker, singer, and composer whose writing on feminism, sexuality, the natural sciences, and metaphysics has appeared in *off our backs, Empathy, Gnosis, Green*

Egg, Jewish Currents, The New Internationalist, and the anthologies *Women's Glib, What's a Nice Girl Like You Doing in a Relationship Like This* (both by Crossing Press), and *Closer to Home: Bisexuality and Feminism* (Seal Press). She is currently working on a book of essays called *The Visionary Feminist.*

Shéree Anne Slaughter is a 35 year old African American, a proud lesbian for 20 years and an established poet. She considers herself a poet with a social cause and enjoys writing serious as well as humorous poems for and about women.

Ann Snitow, a feminist activist since 1970, is a literary critic and essayist. She teaches literature and women's studies at Eugene Lang College and the Graduate Faculty of the New School for Social Research. Her current book project is "A Gender Diary."

Alison Solomon: I wrote this poem after I had made the decision to discontinue infertility treatment. It is sad to think that I could never had made that choice had I stayed in the Indian-Sephardi community in Israel. This poem was written from feelings both of victory and sadness. Victory, because when you have struggled with infertility, making the choice to remain childless, when there are still other options, is courageous and brave. Sadness because infertile women who have chosen neither to let infertility treatment run/ruin our lives, nor to adopt, are not a strong voice in the women's community. Today, eight years later, the victory and the sadness still coexist in me. My life has been more fulfilled than I would ever have imagined ten years ago. I grew up in England and emigrated to Israel at age 18. I came to the States in 1989. Publications include articles in *Infertility: Women Speak Out*, R. Duelli Klein, ed. (London: Unwin Hyman, 1989), *Reproductive and Genetic Engineering: Journal of International Feminist Analysis*, (Pergamon, 1988, 1989) and *Calling the Equality Bluff: Women in Israel*. Sefer, M. & Swirsky, B., eds. (New York: Pergamon, 1991). I am a clinical social worker in Philadelphia, PA.